# The Man who Mistook his Job for his Life

Naomi Shragai

# The Man who Mistook his Job for his Life

How to thrive at work by leaving your emotional baggage behind

WH ALLEN

1

WH Allen, an imprint of Ebury Publishing,
20 Vauxhall Bridge Road,
London SW1V 2SA

WH Allen is part of the Penguin Random House group of companies
whose addresses can be found at global.penguinrandomhouse.com

Penguin
Random House
UK



First published in the United Kingdom by WH Allen in 2021

www.penguin.co.uk

A CIP catalogue record for this book is available from the British Library

Hardback ISBN 9780753558300
Trade Paperback ISBN 9780753558317

Typeset by Jouve (UK), Milton Keynes
Printed and bound in Great Britain by Clays Ltd, Elcograf S.p.A.

The authorised representative in the EEA is Penguin Random House Ireland,
Morrison Chambers, 32 Nassau Street, Dublin D02 YH68

Penguin Random House is committed to a sustainable future for
our business, our readers and our planet. This book is made
from Forest Stewardship Council® certified paper.

FSC
www.fsc.org
MIX
Paper from
responsible sources
FSC® C018179

For my *mensch* of a husband, Charlie

# About the Author

Naomi Shragai graduated from the University of Southern California and completed her training as a systemic psychotherapist at the Tavistock Clinic, London. She has more than 30 years' experience as a psychotherapist and family therapist in private practice, as well as working in the NHS and private hospitals. She now specialises in helping businesses and individuals resolve psychological obstacles that cause work-related problems.

As a freelance journalist she has written for *The Times* and the *Guardian* and since 2008 has been a regular contributor to the *Financial Times*, where she writes predominantly about the psychological aspects of working life. In a previous career, she was a stand-up comic, working on the London comedy circuit as well as making radio and television appearances. She lives in north-west London.

# Author's Note

The names, identities and other features (such as their age, gender and jobs) of my clients featured in this book have been changed and disguised to protect their anonymity. In some cases, composite characters have been created in order to illustrate a general point. I am deeply indebted to them for their generosity and courage in granting permission for their stories to be told.

# Contents

# Introduction: Acting out our internal dramas at work

Do you ever find yourself paralysed by strong feelings at work? Do you overreact to criticism? Do you find yourself responding more like a child than the adult you are with colleagues and bosses? Are you a hardworking, successful person who nonetheless harbours doubts about your competence, despite all the evidence to the contrary?

Such anxieties have only been exacerbated by the seismic changes the world of work has undergone in recent decades, from the digital revolution and demise of the 'job for life' to the new gig economy and, more recently, the #MeToo movement, Black Lives Matter and the coronavirus pandemic. They reflect people's growing emotional and mental investment in their work – something intensified by longer hours, a highly competitive market and an insecure work culture – but they, regrettably, have received sparse attention.

These developments have been reflected in my psychotherapy practice, which I began over 30 years ago and has since developed into a business consultancy. To begin with, I dealt with psychotherapy's traditional subject matter – personal issues and relationship breakdowns. During the past 15 years, however, people have increasingly brought work-related matters to my consulting room. They come with their insecurities of varied forms. Some cannot overcome a compulsion to please others and thereby lose their own creative voice; others struggle with 'impostor syndrome', fearing they are out of their depth in their job. By contrast, some are perfectionists or too controlling and incapable of delegating tasks, both of which undermine business goals and individuals' personal achievement. Others cannot tolerate what they perceive as unfairness in the office, or cope with malicious gossip, cliques or bullying behaviour. Usually, the issue in question is casting a shadow over their happiness, obstructing their career progress and making work feel an unsafe and intolerable place. For many, office relationships have even overtaken family relationships in terms of importance in their lives and the space they take up in their thoughts.

Many who come to see me soon discover that the problems they are facing stem from their childhood experiences. In other words, they find themselves replicating at work the same unwanted family dynamics from their early lives. Once they have come to understand this, the question they ask is: 'Why would I repeat a pattern that makes me so unhappy?' The answer – like so many of the ones you'll encounter in these pages – is surprising but very simple: the pull towards the familiar is strong and it's often powerful enough to overtake our conscious desires. For example, being persistently told off as a child can lead to a fear of rejection by an authority figure. One can become so frightened of making mistakes that thinking becomes paralysed and projects are not completed in time. Eventually, this can trigger the sort of criticism one is trying to avoid. Although returning to the familiar is compelling and can feel comforting, there is no growth to be had in what is known.

Many individuals I have worked with have previously tried to overcome such crippling feelings, negative thoughts and destructive habits using techniques such as positive thinking, reading self-help business books or attending workshops – only to find themselves further entrenched in their problems. In the business world, psychotherapy is rarely an individual's first port of call. And yet, when people are unable to change their thinking and behaviour – or even recognise its origins – while knowing they are harming the company or impairing their career development, the answer, I suggest, is to examine themselves more deeply. The stories I will share from my years as a psychotherapist and business consultant, and the questions I will ask you to consider, will show you how.

It has become common to turn to therapy to recover from personal matters such as depression, grief or divorce and yet rarely do people who find themselves struggling consider such self-examination when it comes to work issues. This may be explained, perhaps, by the lingering false notion that work is a predominantly rational and objective world with specific goals, largely free of emotions. Some may even believe that having a therapist is a mark of weakness or for the 'ill.' They may unconsciously fear what might be revealed. As for companies and organisations, they tend to favour quick, concrete solutions – delivered through assessments, training and courses – rather than taking time to reflect on complexities. Some employers also adhere to the belief that staff should leave their private lives and emotions at home, envisaging workers who are always focused entirely on the job. As Manfred Kets de Vries, the renowned psychoanalyst and professor of leadership development and organisational change at Insead business school, once said to me: 'For many executives, their ideal employee is someone who is just divorced, lives in an empty apartment and takes a sleeping bag and moves into the office to work 24 hours a day.'

The truth is that we all bring our messy emotional lives with us wherever we go, including to work. Alongside our skills, dedication and ambition, we bring to the office our 'inner lives' – our sensitivities, misperceptions, fears and insecurities – the strong emotions that at times hijack us. This includes our unconscious, where we bury the experiences from our early life that we find too painful or uncomfortable to face.

Our families, particularly our earliest relationships, reside deep in our minds and, whether we are aware of it or not, find their way into all our subsequent relationships, including those at work. When we push our painful feelings and experiences from our early years from our awareness they do not disappear but reside in our unconscious where we have no control of them. A common outlet for these repressed memories is that we re-enact our earliest family experiences in the office in such a way that, unconsciously, our managers and colleagues come to resemble our closest relatives. We might, for example, regard a male boss as a father – a current authority figure who represents our earliest authority figure, or the father we wish we had. Or perhaps a dispute with a colleague triggers repressed feelings of when family arguments led to harm and/or rejection because emotions were out of control.

If we were fortunate to have families who responded to our

earliest needs predominantly with warmth, affection and care, then we are likely to anticipate that managers will be interested in us and treat us fairly. If, however, we experienced neglect in our early lives or had parents who harmed us in any way, we are likely to find it difficult to trust colleagues. We might even anticipate that people are against us, attempting to undermine our work or even desire to be rid of us. Paranoid thinking can easily take over.

Without us realising it, our unconscious will keep reappearing and influencing our thoughts and perceptions in ways that can be destructive. In our working lives it can wreak havoc when it acts out unresolved conflicts from the past. Brian, a graphic designer who came to see me, had a fear of authority that he expressed in aggression towards his managers and colleagues – even when they tried to help him. Where did this come from? It turned out he was the son of a single mother who subsequently married and later focused on the two children she had with her husband. Brian had been the centre of his mother's world but, from the age of six, he lost her attention and had to contend with an aggressive and bullying stepfather. He became an outsider – a feeling he subsequently took to work, together with his deep fear and distrust of authority stemming from his relationship with his stepfather.

Acting on repressed experiences rather than actual realities is so often the source of confusion and friction at work. In this way, the office can become a hotbed of irrationality and unresolved disputes. Although our instincts may be useful in spotting irrational behaviour by colleagues, they tend to fail us when we are in the grip of our own internal dramas – when past experiences feel as if they are happening in the present. Until people are willing to appreciate the part they play in creating some of the problems they find themselves in at work, however unconscious, they are unlikely to resolve such career-damaging issues.

The psychological challenges of working life should not be underestimated. It inevitably produces uncomfortable emotions for everyone. Disappointment, frustration, jealousy – even greed and anger feature to a greater or lesser extent. The coronavirus pandemic that began in 2020 compounded such anxieties by forcing much of the working world to work remotely. In the office, if you emerge from a meeting or presentation feeling it went badly, you usually have various people you can talk to for reassurance. Zoom meetings during lockdown ended with blank screens, silence and, most of the time, you, alone in a room. The potential for paranoid thoughts to kick in and escalate unchecked makes it more important than ever for us to take our emotional temperature at work and examine how we can best thrive.

The workplace has, perhaps partly because of our longer hours and the insecurities of modern work, even replaced family life as an arena in which individuals act out their unresolved early conflicts with siblings, parents and other authority figures. Our imagination can be more powerful than actual realities and this is what fuels the contradictions between our inner and outer worlds. Imagined mistakes can feel as bad or worse than an actual mistake and perceived attacks as threatening as real ones.

This all creates greater risks for individuals because

businesses and organisations are less tolerant of emotional behaviour than families. Close personal and family relationships, no matter how fraught, offer more security and allowance for temperamental eruptions. Intimate relationships are concerned with people's well-being, with love and belonging, whereas businesses are about financial success. Although divorce and family breakdown occur, it takes much more strain before people are willing to break such ties. The tolerance of the working world is far less elastic. Business partners can fall out terminally over relatively minor matters; profit falls can result in redundancies and losses cause businesses to be shut down. The risk of rejection, exclusion and failure are higher in business than at home and this creates insecurity and emotional upheaval. This is what my clients want to talk about – the fact that they feel more vulnerable at work.

The insistence on better individual behaviour in recent years has undoubtedly been a force for good in protecting people from bullying, humiliation and sexual or racial harassment. Yet the reduced tolerance for people shouting, losing their temper or bursting into tears, as happens within families, does not allow much room for the fears and emotions underlying such outbursts to be expressed or understood. Often, the consequence of this is people internalising these feelings with the risk of becoming depressed or acting them out in ways that are harmful. When conflicts and strong feelings are not faced, they do not disappear but rather find their ways to hidden corners where they become more destructive. Examples of this are spreading malicious gossip, deliberately missing meetings and withholding ideas that could help colleagues.

Having the emotional maturity to deal with the strong feelings that working life will inevitably stir up is a necessary requirement for success and workplace contentment. Those who have this capacity are often best at navigating office politics, co-operating with colleagues and promoting themselves. For people who struggle with strong feelings, however, the reverse is often true. Bringing our unconscious motivations to conscious awareness where they can be thought about and managed is a crucial part of surviving what our jobs throw at us. Without such awareness, the unconscious is free to act out in ways that are often destructive and undermine our ambitions.

Reading this book will help you sift through the confusion that working life throws at you. You will come to understand why you react strongly, or at times irrationally, to office politics. Making sense of your reactions will lessen the intensity of your feelings and as a result help you make better decisions and collaborate more effectively. You will find yourself more open to feedback, less likely to feel targeted and more willing to hear alternative approaches. This is a natural outcome of understanding how your early experiences and unconscious motivations colour your perception of events in the workplace. Deficiency in this capacity risks misreading situations, reacting impulsively or judging colleagues wrongly.

The aim is also to help you make sense of others' behaviour that appears obstructive, unfair or even mad. Self-awareness will make you better equipped to read both other people and situations accurately, thereby giving you a unique career advantage.

I do not subscribe to a '12 steps to success' formula that many business books promote. Such promises offer an unreal assurance that the same solutions can apply to everyone. Because we all have a unique upbringing and psychological make-up, the answers to the sorts of problems I have outlined will be unique to each of us and we need to take responsibility for finding them.

Many books are aimed at leaders and senior managers; I've chosen instead to focus on the problems most of us face whether we are in positions of power or not. Yet managers will find much to relate to as well. Many newly promoted managers, for example, quickly discover that the skills that helped them achieve their position are no longer relevant, or even harm them, when they reach the top. In their previous position, they were able to keep past internal conflicts at bay but their new role often confronts them with deeper unconscious insecurities. I explore common hindrances to leadership, such as falling into the trap of idealisation, narcissism and failing to delegate.

I explain how early dysfunction in families can, paradoxically, help individuals progress in their career if they are able to develop another trajectory – one that is healthy, creative and transformative. The road to building psychological resilience by learning to tolerate uncomfortable feelings, face harsh realities and develop personal insight, is mapped out. By facing our past and inhibiting the tendency to fall into relational dynamics that are familiar but harmful, we can transform our professional lives for the better.

Our working lives are too long, consuming and potentially life-enriching in every respect to fall victim to self-destruction. Success and satisfaction should be the goals of any career and hopefully reading on will help you meet them.

# 1

# Hijacked by strong feelings – and the defences we mount in the workplace

'Unexpressed emotions will never die. They are buried alive and will come forth later in uglier ways.'

*Sigmund Freud*

The telephone call from Felicity came out of the blue. 'I'm really struggling with work, I know I need help,' she said. I heard the desperation in her voice and offered her my earliest available time.

A week later she arrived at my consulting room, a small, fair-haired, single woman in her early fifties, who had risen to be deputy to the chief executive of an independent financial institution in London. Although she exuded warmth, I noticed a timidity in her character – uncharacteristic, I thought, for someone in her position.

Over the course of our meeting, Felicity described how she was living a double life at work. She had successfully convinced her colleagues that she was calmly able to manage any crisis that came her way – but in fact she had always been plagued by anxiety and insecurities. Indeed, her worry of 'getting it wrong' at work kept her up most nights, even though in the office she was able to project a confident and capable image. As a result, many people brought Felicity their problems and confided in her and so she heard plenty of gossip. This put her in a powerful position. Yet she did not feel powerful. Rather, she felt burdened and fearful of losing her job. Although in a position of authority, she did not feel she had any. It is one thing to 'have' authority and quite another to 'feel' it.

This tension between the image she projected and how she actually felt had become so extreme that Felicity was even unable to take a holiday for fear of what she thought might be revealed in her absence – that she was not needed. Her anxiety about being disregarded was intense, despite continuous affirmations from colleagues and financial rewards in the form of bonuses. Because she could not accept praise, she was stuck in a continuous negative cycle, convinced her only solution was to work hard.

As with many people, her feelings were not based in reality but rather were reactions to insecurities she experienced in early life. She revealed to me that both her parents had behaved selfishly when she was a child and disregarded her needs. Her older brother managed to get their parents' attention because he was the 'problem child,' taking drugs excessively and playing truant from school, while Felicity's more commendable efforts were largely ignored.

'I was a goody two-shoes, while my brother was always getting into trouble and getting the attention,' she told me. 'I thought, "I'll be the good girl, the one who does the right thing and doesn't do drugs." I was the good student, always getting top grades.'

Her efforts proved futile. She never attained the attention

she craved from her parents. Once she even found them smoking cannabis with her brother. His bad behaviour had given him a special relationship with their parents that excluded her. The unfairness of it all made her furious and feel even more disregarded.

Felicity's early experience of being overlooked had left her feeling equally insignificant to her colleagues, which in turn made her work harder to ensure she would not be forgotten. Just as in her childhood, she felt her hard work had been ignored and she was enraged at the unfairness of it all. The situation was exacerbated when her boss became infatuated by an underqualified but attractive – and younger – colleague, whom he promoted ahead of other more deserving candidates, blissfully unaware of the ill feeling this created among his team – and starving Felicity even further of the attention she so craved. History was repeating itself: just as her parents had favoured her brother, her boss was now giving preference to someone who was underperforming.

Just like Felicity, every day that we go to work we take with us two realities. One is the external, actual reality of working lives where we are motivated to achieve, succeed and gain financial rewards. Internally, however, we also bring a different reality, comprising our particular psychological traits, which include our insecurities and misperceptions. A large proportion of this inner reality is our unconscious, home to repressed memories of painful experiences, drives and longings that have their roots in our early lives. Here the agenda is different to that in our external reality: to keep uncomfortable truths and painful memories at bay, for example, or to achieve resolution over unresolved conflicts from the past, as Felicity's story demonstrates.

While she was never able to be the centre of her parents' world, work provided Felicity with another opportunity to be valued, admired and cared about by others and prove that she was, indeed, loveable. Because our two realities have differing aims, they can create internal, and sometimes external, tensions. As long as these inner motivations remain in our unconscious, we have no control over them and when they are in conflict with the external reality, confusion and strong feelings can erupt, which frequently leads to obstacles in our careers and friction with our colleagues.

You will easily be able to identify your conscious motivations at work – for example, to execute a project, improve as a leader, respond to your clients' needs or simply to get to 5pm so you can have a couple of hours off Zoom. So you might be surprised to know that much of what actually motivates our decisions, from the micro to the macro, stems from unconscious attempts to distance ourselves from unpleasant emotions. Take a moment to think about what decisions or actions you have taken that, on reflection, may have been motivated by an attempt to avoid feeling anxious or uncomfortable. Perhaps you avoided calling out an underling for a serious error or acceded to a client's unreasonable demands. Next, consider how you might have responded differently had you been able to *face* those feelings. Now ask yourself: 'What would have been the best course to take for the business and my professional development?'

Being highjacked by strong feelings at work can result in

dire consequences. It can interfere with our capacity to think clearly, to read a situation accurately and ultimately to focus and concentrate on the job. Learning to not just tolerate strong feelings but also understand where they originate and why they upset you is essential in gaining the self-awareness required for professional life. If we could learn to face and *manage* strong feelings and anxieties rather than *avoid* them, we would be better equipped to cope with the minefield of office politics – taking risks, accepting our mistakes and relating to people we find difficult will all be made easier.

Many people find the most difficult part of their job is taking decisions or having conversations that are charged with emotion. They irrationally fear the wrong choice could result in catastrophic consequences. For example, they could imagine that taking a financial risk to expand the company could result in the business failing and this in turn might lead to them becoming poverty stricken. Or they fear being seen as someone who is harsh and critical; and then judged to be a bad person. Many individuals who have come to see me for help have admitted to carrying these unrealistic fears in their minds.

Such fears can envelop our work and many of them are understandable. No one wants to feel awful or be disliked. If we did not expect that others might react badly towards us – reject, ignore or criticise us – we would be free to act in ways that are destructive. The office would be a much more unpleasant place to work, trust would break down and projects less likely to be completed. It is often the anticipation of experiencing shame or guilt that makes us behave better. But it is when our attempts to avoid bad feelings create more problems than they solve, however, that we need to investigate ourselves more deeply.

To protect ourselves at work we attempt to put our best selves forward and this involves 'containing' our negative feelings. Keeping our anger, jealousies and insecurities to ourselves is a useful skill to have. We have all worked alongside people unable to do this and know how unpleasant they make the work environment and how badly they are judged. But if we are able to tolerate uncomfortable emotions rather than acting on them, we are more able to consider what is happening and respond more thoughtfully.

Yet at the same time, some of our emotions reside just beneath the surface in our subconscious and can easily erupt in response to minor events. Such occurrences can throw us off guard when they touch a sensitive chord, feel deeply personal or – as we have seen in the case of Felicity – reactivate traumatic experiences from our past. Perhaps you've noticed your boss smiling at your colleagues but appearing to ignore you. Then, if your idea is dropped at a meeting and you are told it will be on the following week's agenda but it never is, it can leave you disproportionately devastated. Or perhaps the prospect of an annual review keeps you awake at night. Moments like these can ignite strong feelings and cause you to respond more like a child than the adult you are. Irrationality can escalate when emotions grow out of proportion to the actual event and paranoia can even take over.

While we believe our decisions are driven by rational thoughts, more often than not it is our feelings that are leading us. It is much easier to go by our 'gut instincts', how we feel, than to take the time to think things through carefully. Thinking requires time and effort, and often creates confusion or ambivalence, states of mind we prefer to ignore.

Furthermore, our feelings at work have multiple meanings. At one level, we could accept them at face value and allow them to lead us. That is, if we are exhausted, we need to recover; if we are suspicious of a client, perhaps we do need to be more cautious; if we are distraught at not being promoted we might need to work harder. Feelings can be a useful guide, yet they can also mislead. Optimism and desire, for example, can push a project forward but too much can mean signs of dangerous risk are ignored. Pessimism can alert you to potential pitfalls but it can also kill off ideas before they have begun.

When we are hijacked by strong feelings it might mean we are operating more in the past than in the present. Being ignored by your manager is perhaps a reason to be upset but if you flip to rage to the extent that you lose all motivation at work, then you need to examine where those feelings originate. The current circumstances might be triggering repressed feelings from the past when you were treated badly or neglected by your parents. In other words, your feelings are misleading you.

Learning to discriminate between emotions that are trustworthy and those that are misleading is crucial to reading situations correctly, making the best possible decisions and creating good working relationships. This requires us to have an understanding beyond emotional intelligence, by which I mean empathy, self-regulation and social skills. We must also learn the kind of self-awareness that helps us to separate the past from the present and bring our unconscious drives to conscious awareness. Felicity, for example, when recognising that her anxieties and rage originated in her early family life, was gradually able to bear these feelings.

Many people who come to me are surprised to learn that feelings can be kept to oneself and thought about, rather than necessarily acted on; that is, they can be *understood* and *managed.* Some people believe that having strong feelings is proof of their 'rightness' and entitles them to act as they please. On the contrary, when feelings are out of proportion to an event, it is more likely the individual has distorted reality and is responding to historic events or internal states.

It is not only our emotions that influence our decisions and behaviour in the workplace, we can also be led by *imagined* scenarios rather than *actual* ones. Learning to tell these realities apart is an important step. Keep in mind, however, that an imagined reality can feel as powerful, or even more so, than the actual, or external, one. If our imagined reality leaves us feeling highly anxious, our jobs can become unnecessarily intolerable. Convincing ourselves, for example, that we will be judged harshly for minor mistakes may lead us to work needless long hours in order to avoid criticism. Or if we believe we have to 'do it alone' in order to succeed, we might miss offers of help and shows of support.

In short, the workplace is a psychological melting pot with a vast array of hidden emotions in play as each individual brings their internal life to the office. With everyone acting out, to a greater or lesser extent, their early family lives, it is no wonder relationships can be fraught and emotions run high. Stir in also the stress of competition, insecure work cultures and overworking, and it is a triumph, I sometimes think, that work is ever done efficiently and businesses succeed despite all the irrational thinking and behaviour. It is to the credit of staff, managers and leaders who are able to navigate this minefield and still produce results.

The ability to separate the external reality from our internal dramas is crucial to business success. Becoming aware of our feelings marks the beginning of our journey to emotional maturity, though awareness by itself is not enough. The next step is what I call 'inhibition' – identifying the source of thinking that leads to misguided perceptions and then holding back your reactions. This will allow you time to reflect and assess the situation more accurately, giving you the mental space to determine whether you are reacting to internal or external events. Finding the time to reflect is a challenge when one is facing deadlines, under constant pressure to perform and having to navigate persistent disruptions. Yet thinking about such matters will save you time in the long run because you are not creating unnecessary problems.

Initial insight, however, is not the end of the story. Change requires persistent vigilance in recognising and inhibiting defensive reactions. Responding to what is actually happening time and time again will help to create new pathways of understanding and responding. Growth occurs where we put our attention. When we attend to historic and unhealthy patterns, they continue to become ingrained but if we focus on new and creative responses, so our healthy side develops.

Although this process is often slow and inconsistent, when insights occur they seep through our conscious minds, leading to deep shifts in perception. Gradually your view of events will begin to alter. People who seemed impossible to collaborate with suddenly appear approachable. A change of work routine that might have left you anxious feels manageable. You recover from setbacks more quickly. These changes occur naturally as a result of persistently paying attention to your perceptions, feelings and reactions. And once we have enough self-awareness to overcome the hurts and blows of office life, the disappointment of failures, the humiliation of mistakes, we still have to extend ourselves further and appreciate that everyone comes to work with their emotional baggage – their irrationalities, misperceptions and bad behaviour. It is not just you – everyone is bringing their past into their present.

Perhaps if Felicity had made the link between her reactions at work and her early life, she would have been able to regard her job differently and find the courage to report her boss to human resources. Her team, in turn, would have felt safer knowing that such impropriety was taken seriously. The experience of standing up for herself and her staff would have helped her develop a sense of genuine internal authority. Instead, her unconscious overrode her conscious mind and rather than asserting her authority she regressed to feeling like a child. Rather than creating a new trajectory she repeated a familiar one.

Her story also demonstrates the psychological strategies, or defence mechanisms, that people use to ward off anxieties and emotions they find excruciating. The term 'defence mechanisms' has negative connotations for many people and they use it critically, such as 'she is so defensive', implying the person is either aggressive or not hearing what is being said – or both. The implication here is that defences are maladaptive and harmful.

While there is a negative side to defence mechanisms, they have an immensely positive function as well. They protect us from strong and threatening feelings such as shame, grief, envy or rage. Defence mechanisms are, for the most part, healthy and normal and we all rely on them to varying extents to manage our emotional lives and make the world more tolerable. Without such mechanisms, we would be so overwhelmed by powerful feelings that we could not function in our jobs.

There are different types of defence mechanisms and while all intend to protect the individual from actual or perceived threats, some are more rigid than others. 'Reaction formation', for example, is the mind's way of turning an unacceptable trait into its opposite in order to feel less threatened. Felicity attempted to cover what she believed were her negative traits – weakness and insecurity – by conveying an air of calm and confidence. Furthermore, she sought the attention she received only fleetingly from her parents by making herself needed and even indispensable to colleagues. Sadly, and paradoxically, her approach made it less likely she would receive such support and validation because her mask of competence and composure made colleagues think this was the last thing she needed. Instead, she only managed to re-enact an unhappy pattern from childhood.

Her boss, meanwhile, used 'denial,' another common defence mechanism, which fends off bad feelings such as guilt and shame. Denial – the refusal to accept a situation – can help us through initial moments of a crisis, such as in sudden grief when we say to ourselves: 'This cannot be true.' In its less benign forms, however, the refusal to accept serious realities can lead to catastrophic outcomes for individuals and organisations. This was certainly the case for Felicity's chief; he was eventually sacked for his amorous behaviour.

Another defence mechanism is 'splitting,' in which only good news is accepted while the bad is pushed from one's awareness. Splitting is a reaction to our intolerance of the tension and confusion triggered by emotional complexity. This technique helps resolve this tension by simplifying a situation as either all good or all bad, expelling any ambiguity or ambivalence. For example, if it is confusing that one both admires and resents one's boss because of their various characteristics, the negative or hostile feelings could be strong enough to wipe out the positive ones, making the relationship seem intolerable. However, if one can simultaneously be conscious of one's admiration as well, the boss will suddenly seem not so bad after all. If you frequently conclude that circumstances or people are either totally good or bad, you need to learn to live in the grey areas that more accurately reflect reality. Equally, seeing the bad in others and only the good in ourselves, or vice versa, is damaging. An example is when we blame a colleague entirely for a failure, neglecting to take responsibility for our part, or in contrast we overestimate our actions and become devastated.

Splitting can also involve pushing aside, or splitting off, one's own negative traits, such as manipulation, weakness or aggression, and perceiving these qualities in another person – a process called 'projection'. Through projection, yet another defence mechanism, we rid ourselves of feelings or qualities we dislike in ourselves by attributing them to others. People who rely on this can often end up blaming or bullying the person they have wrongly accused in an attempt to eliminate these traits entirely.

While these mechanisms may sound irrational, if not taken to extremes they clearly have a beneficial effect. It is unlikely you could cope with the demands of your job without employing some of them. Telling yourself that an issue is not nearly as bad as it actually is – 'rationalisation' – helps you cope with what otherwise might be overwhelming. Taking out your resentments towards your manager by being short tempered at home – a mechanism known as 'displacement' – might help to avoid conflicts in the office. 'Intellectualisation' can be another defence, as it helps remove the emotional overload that interferes with rational decision making by focusing on thinking rather than feeling. Sometimes cold, hard decisions that hurt people are required for the overall good.

Most people manage well by using these mechanisms sparingly. They allow us to focus under extreme stress and to contain feelings when it would be inappropriate to express them. The more rigid the defence mechanism, however, such as denial, the further reality is distorted and the more likely you are to misread situations and create problems as a result. Furthermore, these mechanisms eventually break down and one is left facing an issue neglected for too long. Avoiding taking a decision or action, for example, because it makes us anxious, leaves us with more to deal with, not less. Facing the truth that one has made a 'bad hire' when recruiting someone can be difficult. It is easier to convince oneself that the person is 'not too bad really' or that 'he'll get better with experience' than to prepare for a turbulent time ahead and face clearing up a bigger mess.

So our defence mechanisms at work have their uses but also their dangers and limitations. Particularly as one climbs the career ladder, defensive strategies that have previously kept bad feelings at bay are no longer efficient. With increased responsibility and more complex interpersonal relationships to manage, the limitations of one's defence mechanisms are exposed. Pushing blame on others as a way to escape responsibility, for example, or being in denial about crucial issues creates bigger problems at senior levels.

Another consideration is that when your defences are too rigid, they not only shut out bad feelings but also positive ones necessary to boost your career. People who over-intellectualise, for example, are often detached from their emotions and gut instincts, which are useful in relating to colleagues, navigating office politics and being creative.

Although we might be aware of some our defensive strategies, the most destructive ones remain beyond our conscious awareness and this is what makes it difficult to control our reactions. For example, rationalisation or displacement may be easier to spot than denial or reaction formation, which are more ingrained and unconscious. It is also far easier to identify defensive reactions in our colleagues and managers than to recognise them in ourselves. In fact, we are likely to become defensive when these traits are pointed out to us and then miss opportunities to develop. If you react badly to feedback, it would be wise to think about why it has touched you so deeply. Talking it over with someone you trust, either outside or inside your workplace, might shed light on it. We need to be vigilant of our reactions to circumstances to gain conscious control over these processes. Too often, it is only when these mechanisms break down or when a crisis occurs that they become apparent.

We all have to wear a mask in our public lives to some extent so as not to expose our deepest vulnerabilities. Convincing others of our confidence and ability to perform is necessary to maintain our position and climb the career ladder. Although essential, this mask means that we all carry a tension between the image we convey and our actual thoughts and feelings. When this tension becomes extreme, as it had for Felicity, it can lead to obsessive thoughts of what might happen should the inner self be exposed.

It is useful to think of yourself as having 'parts' – that is, while a part of yourself is trying to resolve a historic event, another part is determined to deal with the present. For example, your job might require that you show creativity and though a part of you is determined to succeed, another fears expressing ideas that might elicit a negative response. Perhaps somewhere in your past you were humiliated in this regard, at home or school, and the prospect of re-experiencing that ridicule is too awful to contemplate. Does this mean that you fear success? Not entirely. It suggests that part of you is anxious about reliving those humiliating feelings even while another is determined to do well. You are in conflict. The unconscious part, if not understood and managed, could easily undermine the conscious part.

Acknowledging that various parts reside in you is liberating – when you know that your insecure or immature parts do not define you entirely it makes them easier to bear and helps you to forge a way forward. Learning how to access the healthier parts helps you manage the unconscious or more harmful ones.

Take time to consider how your emotional life accompanies you to work. What defensive strategies might you unconsciously deploy to avoid uncomfortable feelings? Pause for a moment and consider the questions below. Keep in mind there are no 'right' answers – they are simply to encourage you to reflect. Allow your mind to wander. If incidents arise from other aspects of your life, see if you can make connections where you hadn't before. Look for patterns between the past and present, or between your home and professional lives. Separating past events from present ones will keep you grounded in the here and now.

- Do you overcompensate for traits you dislike about yourself? Perhaps, for instance, appearing confident to cover feelings of inadequacy?
- Have you taken anger out on someone who doesn't deserve it? This is characteristic of displacement.
- Do you tend to write people off if they upset you? This is characteristic of splitting.

- Are you especially harsh on people who have traits you dislike in yourself, such as weakness, neediness or greed? This is characteristic of projection.
- How do you react to critical feedback at work? Are you often defensive? Do you personalise feedback?

A friend of mine, after discussing this subject, once said to me in a voice heavy with frustration: 'It's so hard to be human, isn't it?' She is right. We all have our fears and vulnerabilities. The following chapters, however, aim to ease this burden somewhat.

2

# The impostor syndrome – or, when feeling a fraud can be a blessing

'I felt that someone would say, "What are you doing here?" and I'd be going, "Well, I'm just trying to get it done. I'm not fully in control of everything. I'm making the best of what I can." I definitely had this feeling that [the boss] was going to say: "Come on William, you're not any good at this, go and do something else."'

'There were times I'd go to work and feel like there was a great big pressure on my chest. I was always scared I was going to miss something – had I read the latest email or if someone called me would I fuck it up? That's how it felt. But people said to me: "You always looked like you were in complete control of what was going on." Well, it didn't feel like it to me – it felt like chaos, and chaos is exhausting.'

William's frank and moving words get to the heart of the impostor syndrome. His was an extreme case and one I will return to later, but it is not what people usually think of whenever I mention the syndrome. Their response is usually along the lines that 'everyone has it.' There is a degree of truth in this. Undoubtedly, almost everyone will at times feel a fraud and experience the dread of being outed as not up to the job. We all need to 'fake it till we make it' to some extent because our careers depend on convincing others of our competence and confidence. Keeping up appearances is normal and natural. How one experiences these feelings, however – where they originate or whether they are helpful or harmful in our working lives – varies widely from person to person.

Typically people with impostor syndrome dismiss any success as simply luck or having the right contacts or personal charm. They are unable to recognise their achievements and believe they are undeserved. Sadly, such individuals are unable to gain satisfaction from work and often sabotage their professional development. Even if they are performing well, they worry they are only as good as their last accomplishment, rather than seeing their success as a product of cumulative experience and achievements.

There are likely to be rising numbers of such people in a world of rapid change in technology and the working environment, combined with the uncertainty and inevitable anxiety this creates. With increasing intolerance of mistakes and failures, and people constantly being put into new roles, the feeling of being out of one's depth is undoubtedly more prevalent than in the past. Social media are also responsible for creating an image-dominant culture where people are relentlessly encouraged to put their best self forward. Seeing others' glossy images of their lives, scrubbed clean of any taint or setback, only heightens awareness of our own weaknesses and increases the pressure to cover them up.

Many attempt to simplify this syndrome by suggesting we all share similar symptoms and complaints. Yet the impostor syndrome stretches along a lengthy continuum from mild discomfort and doubts, which can be tolerated and even helpful, to the more extreme end, which has the potential to harm one's effectiveness, career and even damage a business. It is when the experience changes from the occasional awareness of feeling a fraud to it dictating one's decisions and behaviour – such as refusing a promotion, avoiding necessary risks or procrastinating to the point where nothing gets done – that it becomes a problem.

Few are immune entirely to this predicament. It strikes people across the professional range, from low pay grades to middle managers and even – and especially – chief executives and other leaders. Some hope that experience and promotion will offer an escape but with added responsibility comes more visibility, which in turn can lead to further self-doubt and the ensuing need to hide it. Another challenge for people elevated to leadership positions is that they move further away from their established skills. Individuals are promoted because they shine at their profession or trade but this does not mean they necessarily possess management or leadership skills. Their training and expertise in previous positions become irrelevant and what is now required is more about dealing with people. But it is often the earlier roles that provided them with a sense of competence, confidence and personal identity. Suddenly their technical skills have become redundant and they are having to deal with a changed role and interpersonal challenges. In their previous positions their job may have offered more tangible results and evidence of success, such as completing a project, making a sale or gaining a high return on investments. In a more senior position, there are fewer such concrete rewards on offer and fewer ways to mark achievements.

The gap between one's self-perception and the perception of others is even greater as one reaches the top and this can leave individuals feeling worse and more isolated. As a result, they find leadership, with its increased exposure, adding to their impostor discomfort. They cannot take pleasure in their success; instead it becomes a burden as they struggle to stay afloat rather than cresting the waves. Such feelings are normal when beginning an unfamiliar and challenging role. It only becomes problematic when the anxiety fails to subside after a reasonable period.

It should be said that sometimes individuals see fault in themselves when in fact their organisation has unrealistically high expectations. Just as abused children will blame themselves rather than accept that people who are meant to look after them are harming them, so can employees accept failure as their own rather than acknowledge that the employer is making unrealistic demands. These are often dependent personalities who need to see their employer as all-good and all-caring in order to feel secure. Indeed, organisations, when not allowing for failures or mistakes, or having excessively high expectations of staff, must shoulder much responsibility for the growth of this syndrome.

Let's examine this impostor syndrome continuum more closely, beginning at the mild end. Here, humility, modesty and a willingness to show vulnerability are useful as they help people warm to you and can defuse resentment and potential envy from colleagues. Insecurity also makes us more likely to prepare well for work tasks, to focus on details and be more aware of potentially dangerous risks. In short, some fear of being found out makes us work harder and therefore more likely to succeed. We are also less likely to make bad decisions because we think through issues more carefully.

The opposite traits of arrogance and being a 'know-it-all' can repulse colleagues and reduce the likelihood of gaining their support. Such characteristics also imply that one believes there is nothing to learn and no self-development required, factors that might even lead to a loss of motivation. Such a mindset is far more limiting than fearing being a fraud.

Farrah Storr, author of the book *The Discomfort Zone*, says women need to appreciate that the impostor syndrome can be a gift rather than an excuse to hold them back. In her view, this is what lies behind women's proactive approach to learning, why they handle the stress of job interviews better, why they prepare more and take fewer risks and why women's investment returns outperform men's. Feeling fraudulent, she says, is a sign you are being challenged and this is what spurs individuals to learn and grow.

A top investor from a leading hedge fund came to realise that his self-doubt is the secret weapon behind his successful investments. He put it to me this way: 'I'm second-guessing myself all the time. [Self-doubt] is a strength for my investing but a hindrance to my leadership.' He fears that changing his mindset would not only undermine his talent but also his way of charming people.

A touch of impostor syndrome can also be healthily realistic. Ignoring traits in ourselves that are difficult to accept leads to blind spots. Pushing unwanted characteristics out of our awareness makes it more likely we will project the same traits on to others. Facing one's limitations is as important as acknowledging your achievements. It prompts you to think about aspects of yourself that need attention – self-destructive traits that need curbing or a skill that needs improving, whether it be regarding organisational matters, communication or collaboration. It might lead you to seek advice or help from a mentor, coach or even a therapist. Awareness of one's weaknesses and fallibilities can also help you to be more realistic about expectations for yourself and let others know what they can expect from you. This can strengthen you for potential future setbacks or failures. With the knowledge that you can bear such feelings, you are more likely to accept and even enjoy fresh challenges that catapult you from your comfort zone.

For individuals at the milder end, their motivations are more likely to be based on external realities – perhaps the knowledge that their skills need improvement. Beginning a new role inevitably breeds anxiety. This is only natural. The other end of the continuum, however, is a darker and more destructive place. There, the more neurotic sufferer's motivations are likely to originate from their internal world and early life. While the milder sufferer's concern is more fear of failure, underlying the more neurotic insecurities may even be an unconscious fear of success, of which more later.

The imposter syndrome manifests in behavioural symptoms from mild to destructive. Someone towards the midway of the spectrum might seek reassurance from colleagues, which can be helpful. However, if they make excessive demands on others to validate their performance, their colleagues become irritated and back away, and needed support is lost. At the more destructive end, a bigger pitfall is inhibition of creativity, which requires exposing and sharing ideas. Similar fears prevent individuals taking necessary risks. Catastrophic scenarios play out in one's mind and the imagined outcomes stop decisions and actions from happening before they begin. It can be so extreme as to paralyse thinking. Such limitations stunt professional growth and may also harm the person's company or organisation. Being unable to bank and value their achievements, people on the more extreme end cannot build on their successes and accumulatively feel better about themselves. One setback has the potential to wipe out all previous successes.

The risk for business and organisation leaders is highlighted by Manfred Kets de Vries, the psychoanalyst and leadership expert, in his book *The Leader on the Couch*. 'More dangerous, however, is neurotic imposture's effect on the quality of decision making. Executives who feel like impostors are afraid to trust their own judgement. Their fearful, overly cautious kind of leadership can easily spread across the company and bring about dire consequences for the organisation. For instance, a neurotic impostor CEO is very likely to suppress his company's entrepreneurial capabilities. After all, if he doesn't trust his own instincts, why should he trust anyone else's?'

Kets de Vries also points out that CEOs in the grip of acute imposter syndrome are highly likely to become addicted to outside consulting companies to help them make decisions because reassurances provided by 'impartial' outsiders compensate for the executive's feelings of insecurity.

This is one way people defend against extreme feelings of

fraudulence. The most common defence mechanisms, however, are perfectionism and workaholism. Sufferers will go to whatever extremes necessary to avoid mistakes, such is their anxiety. Typically, these people frustrate colleagues because they double-check every piece of work to the extent that projects are badly delayed. Imagined mistakes can feel as bad, or worse, than actual ones. This leads to an alternative defensive strategy: procrastination. In the individual's mind, the imagined outcome is so catastrophic that starting a course of action feels near to impossible.

Many tips and techniques for overcoming the impostor syndrome have been suggested in books and articles. 'Share your burden,' 'stop comparing yourself with others,' 'remember your accomplishments,' 'never say no,' are just some of them. Undoubtedly, these are helpful but if such advice does not assist you in overcoming your anxieties, a more profound search to find their origins is required. The underlying, often unconscious factors need to be addressed.

I would argue that for more neurotic sufferers, the seeds have been planted early in their career and, for some, in early life. Again, it is when unresolved conflicts from the past are confused with events in the workplace that this syndrome is unlikely to be resolved easily. Overcoming such anxieties requires you to first consider where you reside on this spectrum and then try to understand how your early experiences led you there.

For Kathy, a 32-year-old successful marketing executive for a retail store chain, it was a crisis in her relationship that brought her to seek help. She travelled by train for her first visit to my consulting room in north-west London. The ten-minute walk from the nearest station is along a leafy street lined with mansion houses predominantly divided into individual flats and provides a useful opportunity for clients to gather their thoughts before seeing me.

During her first session she smiled a lot but her smile seemed unnatural and I suspected there was more behind its facade. She dressed casually and, although this passed the professional mark, I suspected that she did not give undue attention to her appearance. Friendly and outgoing, she was about to tackle therapy with an apparently confident approach and an 'I don't really need anyone's help, thank you' attitude.

She began her story, telling me her boyfriend complained that her workaholism, coupled with a lack of warmth and intimacy, was endangering the relationship. In subsequent sessions it became apparent that unless she was willing to tackle her workaholism there would be little chance of the relationship surviving. Like many workaholics, she preferred to concentrate on achieving in her career than deal with the mess of intimacy. Whereas at work she was able to keep her personal self hidden behind the boundaries of working life, intimacy made her anxious. While she could excel in her career, her personal life was a constant source of worry and conflict.

'For me, work is a structured place – you're able to do your job and you know what's expected of you,' she explained. 'I've always been very guarded about who I am at work and who I let people see. I may not let anyone know what's going on in my personal life because I don't want that to be used against me. Part of it is because I'm a woman. I don't want people to think differently of me – to say if I haven't been feeling brilliant it's because of my menstrual cycle . . . I don't allow it to happen.'

Although Kathy was well educated, having excelled at school and gained a first in her university degree, she nevertheless doubted herself constantly. Achieving promotions and other rewards at work did little to quell her fears of getting it wrong. Her expectation of having to know it all left her terrified to ask for help.

'It's not a lack of ability, it's questioning your own ability and whether what you're doing is right. If I rationalise it, of course I'm good enough, but it's in that moment of not knowing – not necessarily having the confidence to put my hand up and say I don't know some things.'

Her rational side did little to ease her anxieties. Indeed, her fears overtook it and exacerbated her workaholic and perfectionistic tendencies. The cost of her perfectionism was high – her expectations extended to the team she managed, on whom she imposed the same unrealistic demands.

'I strive for everything to be right,' she said. 'I don't like it when everything isn't and I expect everyone to have that same level of perfectionism that I have and I really struggle when people don't.'

She micromanaged her junior staff, involving herself in details that should have been left to them.

'It is yourself that you're protecting here rather than your staff,' I suggested. 'It is their errors you believe will reflect badly on you.' It was clear from her reaction that my words had hit home.

Her close monitoring denied them an opportunity to make mistakes, learn and develop their own style. Imposing harsh standards on staff is one of the more damaging aspects of the impostor syndrome.

Kathy was caught in a cycle of unrealistic expectations she imposed on herself, followed by extreme perfectionism and workaholism to achieve those goals. When she fell short, rather than adjust her expectations, she worked harder and the cycle only repeated itself. This is a common pattern and explains why people at the destructive end of the syndrome are at high risk of burnout when they fail to rein in their perfectionistic tendencies.

Although she worked long and hard hours, Kathy was satisfied with what she was able to achieve and was unlikely to change. It took the need to rescue her relationship to motivate her to deal with these entrenched habits.

Kathy told me about her background. She was the eldest of three sisters raised on a deprived housing estate in north-east England. When she was seven, her father, who suffered mental illness, left home. He was illiterate but it was primarily because of his illness that he was unable to work. Her mother often had three jobs at a time to support the family, which meant she was regularly absent. Nevertheless, her mother stressed the importance of education and Kathy soon discovered doing well at school would win her mother's attention.

'Because my parents weren't there to guide us, direct us or talk to us, we had to find our own way. The one thing from when I was younger [was that] I always had to go to school and there was more interest in achievement academically. I remember feeling proud to achieve and I tried to follow that through.'

Kathy worked hard to grasp any moment of interest from her mother and later this would propel her to achieve professionally.

'I remember feeling really joyful to share the academic results with my mum. She had such a busy life she wasn't able to be interested in the normal day-to-day stuff because she wasn't there. No one cared what time I got up, what time I dressed, no one was there – you had to do it yourself.'

While her mother was hardworking and held high academic expectations for her children, Kathy watched her father's life deteriorate as his mental health worsened. Subconsciously, she feared that if she did not live up to her mother's work ethic her life might follow her father's sad course. So any weakness needed to be covered up. At work, she overcompensated by being industrious and perfectionistic. Showing any failing, she feared, would be the beginning of her life unravelling like her father's.

She feared that asking for help would reveal that she was weak or 'stupid', or expose her as not capable, and so she became self-sufficient. However, there was a cost to hiding her vulnerability at work.

'People think I'm more distant than I really am. They think that I get on with my own stuff and don't want help, when actually I would like help but I would like help in a certain way. I take too much responsibility for everything and I shouldn't.'

Yet while it's possible to maintain this cover at work,

personal relationships are about showing needs, being close and thereby fostering a sense of belonging and love – and this is where she struggled. The cost to her well-being and personal life was high.

'I won't exercise. I'll end up staying late so I'm tired. I won't take the time to prepare myself a nice meal, or any meal. Instead, I'll pull something together and get on with work. I've chosen to put my attention into work rather than my boyfriend.'

Because Kathy could not tolerate inadequacies in herself, she projected it on to others – sometimes underlings at work, colleagues or even her boss – but more often it was her partner who was landed with unwanted characteristics. In him, she saw her useless father and she also attempted to rid herself of the 'neediness' she could not bear in herself by attributing it to him. So, unable to be intimate with her partner, work had become an alternative place to make connections and to create pseudo close relationships. The structure of the working environment allowed a place where she would not be alone but where relationships could feel tolerable as they did not come with the demands of intimacy. The insights revealed in our sessions helped her to recognise the unfair accusations she projected on to her boyfriend and so began her attempts to show more vulnerability at home. In the office, she had to tone down her unrealistic expectations of her staff.

Incidentally, Kathy is also an example of a trap that people frequently fall into that I call 'failed solutions.' This means persevering with a solution to a problem that is clearly not working and which in fact only worsens it. Her favoured solution to her anxiety was overworking but it only made her more anxious. Yet rather than stopping and reflecting on this and thinking of alternative remedies, she resorted to more of the same – working harder. The underlying factors behind her behaviour became further entrenched and eventually workaholism became the problem itself. In short, the attempted solution had become the problem. How was she ever going to break this cycle?

We'll come back to Kathy but I want now to consider another common underlying motivation behind impostor syndrome: feeling guilty and undeserving of success. William, whose sad reflections on his working life we heard at the beginning of this chapter, is an example of this. He is a tall, gentle giant of a man in his mid-forties, married with three children. He cut his engineering career short because of crippling fears of not being capable enough. Unable to accept the praise given to him by colleagues, he dismissed his achievements, burying them under extreme feelings of inadequacy. His financial success was the one thing that counteracted his feelings of fraudulence.

'Money is important to me,' he said. 'You can't argue that £100,000 isn't more than £50,000. I go for money as a way to prove to myself that I am successful.'

Eventually, however, even this broke down when he began to feel guilty. 'I felt I was being paid too much money and I wasn't worth it. Why should I earn more than a teacher?'

His father was a workaholic who sacrificed being an attentive father for his career. As a result, William never received the recognition he craved from his father and most attempts to gain his attention went awry.

'Looking back, my parents weren't there for me in an educational way,' he reflected. 'They didn't support or encourage and they certainly didn't praise. My father was not absent but mentally he wasn't engaged with us. It went beyond that – there was no recognition that I was achieving a lot in sport, that I was doing very well academically. He had extremely high standards for himself and for me but he provided no support. And no recognition when I did succeed – that was quite impactful on me when going into work.'

As a result, he pushed his parents away. 'I wanted the recognition from my parents around achievement and when I didn't get it I said, "I don't want it". When Dad said he couldn't come to my graduation because he had a business meeting and Mum said she would come, I said, "No, I don't want you to come". I was really pissed off.'

His craving to be close to his father never ceased, however, and this ultimately drove him to follow in his footsteps and become an engineer. As a child, he found the one way he could engage with his father was by discussing technical things. Yet because his parents were high achievers, he believed he could never rise to their standards. Observing his parents sacrifice their social and family life to excel academically and professionally, he became convinced that success comes with a price.

'I saw the negative effects of success; it meant that [my father] couldn't spend time with the family and I was hurt by that.'

He was determined instead to focus on his creative talents and personal relationships. At university, he put his energy into playing in a band rather than into his degree and pushed his longings to gain his father's attention out of his mind and into his unconscious.

'You desperately want recognition from your father but you're not going to get it – and so you do not want to play that game,' he told me forcefully. 'I was committed to doing my degree but I didn't spend my energy trying to get a first-class degree. I absolutely felt I'm only going to be second rate – and that spilled out into other students; I felt they were going to be better than me.'

It is an ironic truth that what you reject you take as your own and this was the case for William. While he consciously believed he had given up on his father, he had instead internalised the man who was so harsh on him to become someone who was harsh on himself. Our family is our first experience of the world and this creates a template for how we imagine others will respond to us. In William's case, he anticipated that working life would not offer him recognition or support because his parents had not provided this. Ignoring voices that offered praise, he listened only to his internal voice, which repeatedly stressed he was not good enough, he didn't belong and eventually he would be found out.

'You tend to beat yourself up for things you do wrong really badly and then beat yourself up for the things you do right because it was just a bit of luck or you should have done better than that. I would compare myself with the strongest performer in my peer group and say, "I'm not as good as that person doing that." I'll choose a colleague's best trait and say, "I'm not as good as they are at that."'

Perhaps if his father had given fleeting praise, William might have strived harder. It would have planted a seed in his mind that if he tried hard enough, he might eventually gain the endorsement he craved. But such praise never came. The cost to him was high. It limited his career progress; he was unable to find satisfaction in his work and his fears made him feel terrible much of the time. He would even turn compliments from his boss into criticism – 'He is just saying that because he wants to keep me going but at some point he's going to push me away.' Confusing his boss for his father, he desperately craved validation from him but it was either not forthcoming or he was unable to recognise it. That left him with the same feelings he had as a boy and William's plaintive words at the start of this chapter could easily have come from that child: 'I felt that someone would say "What are you doing here?" and I'd be going, "Well, I'm just trying to get it done. I'm not fully in control of everything. I'm making the best of it I can." I definitely had this feeling which was he [the boss – or perhaps his father] was going to say, "Come on William you're not any good at this, go and do something else."'

He hid it well, as former colleagues observed after he had quit engineering: 'You always looked like you were in complete control of what was going on,' they said. But underneath there was that 'great big pressure on my chest,' work 'felt like chaos, and chaos is exhausting.'

Although he recognised his talents in interpersonal relationships, he was never able to change the trajectory of his career for a more rewarding one. His inability to seek help had made it more difficult to change. Just as encouragement and support had been lacking from his family, he could neither recognise nor access this from colleagues and managers.

Another reason why William, like so many individuals, had not been able to resolve this syndrome is offered by Michael Bader, a psychoanalyst and writer, who believes the core issue is actually a form of guilt. While it feels like a fear of failure or humiliation, unconsciously, a fear of success underlies this syndrome.

According to Dr Bader, while more people are aware of the feelings of shame and humiliation, they are less conscious of the underlying fears of success and deeper guilt. With more success comes more exposure and more to be anxious about, while failure actually provides a 'get-out clause' that can offer some relief and hope they can escape such crippling feelings. For some people, undermining their career through a failure to delegate, for instance, brings about the failure they unconsciously seek in order to escape. Furthermore, he argues that many of us hold an unconscious belief that we are not supposed to have more of life's good things than our parents, or the people who looked after us. Some of these benefits include power, authority and expertise. A conflict develops, he says, because at the same time we are also ambitious and seek to develop, exercise our competence and succeed.

'We do so, but then pay the price with a sense of fraudulence. Or it leads us to fail to take legitimate pleasure and pride in our very real accomplishments. It leads some people to sabotage themselves when they get power, almost as if they are punishing themselves and thereby reducing the conflict between their ambitions and their guilt.'

Ultimately, this is a form of 'survivor guilt', a concept originally applied to those who survived a disaster of some kind and who often spend the rest of their lives making themselves, and others, miserable as a punishment for surviving where others perished. Yet survivor guilt is a much broader phenomenon and applies to the irrational belief that by having any of life's good things – including success – others will be hurt or depleted. People suffering this may even worry about potential retaliation from envious others. Will people resent their success? Will they find themselves excluded and alone?

Many men such as William locate the origin of their feelings of fraudulence in their relationship with fathers who were demanding, harsh and critical, or ignored them. Some seek to gain their father's approval through success but then cannot accept their achievements because the validation is not coming from their father. Alternatively, they feel guilty for having surpassed their father.

Dr Bader told me: 'These are punishment fantasies for the "crime" of being more successful than the father, or being different than the father, or working less hard than the father, or enjoying work more than anyone in the family. Being confident, relaxed in one's sense of competence and feeling entitled to praise all symbolically represent surpassing and/or separating from one's father.'

Another example comes from Ted, a 46-year-old who, significantly, began his own business only three months after his father died. Only after some years had Ted come to understand how his unconscious guilt for surpassing his father's quality of life held him back. His father had been abandoned by his mother at birth and spent his working life as a manual labourer.

He said: 'There's a sadness in distancing myself from him. I feel responsible for the distress he had being abandoned as a baby. The baby got left, stage one, and somewhere landed in my arms. Somewhere, I decided I can't leave the baby.'

British playwright and director Patrick Marber was asked in an interview for the *Observer* newspaper in 2020 what his father's job was.

'He wanted to do what I do – to be a director, a writer, a comedy person. He was director of light entertainment at the BBC but ended up working in the City [of London]. He was amiably jealous of my career. I always felt guilty I'd achieved what he couldn't. It was complicated. I can say it now because he is dead . . . it was a bit of a Freudian nightmare.'

Women, Dr Bader says, have significant survivor guilt, more often in relationship to their mothers. It reflects unconscious prohibitions against being happier, sexier and more successful with men, and with their careers. If mothers have sacrificed their career to raise their children, their daughters feel guilt about having a more fulfilling life.

One woman I talked to, Jenny, had not returned to work after having children because she had lost her confidence, even though she was desperately unhappy as a stay-home mother. Guilt that her career could harm her family also constrained her. Her parents were working class and had missed out on a university education. Jenny's mother resented staying at home to look after her children and made her feelings known. Jenny was the first in her family to attend university and later moved to London, where she found a fulfilling job in public relations. Yet her gains, she concluded, were her mother's losses. Jenny's sophisticated lifestyle, opinions, even her accent became far removed from her parents' and her mother could not bear the distance between them. She was hurt and resentful about her daughter's new-found career.

'With my mother, I felt there was always a tension between being proud and being resentful,' Jenny said. 'It was in the way she described my work; she would say, "Jenny landed herself in a job and gets taken to lunch and picked up in a limousine," as if it's easy. She acted as if I just waltzed into it – as if all you need to do is show up. She would say sarcastically, "Oh, the decadence!"'

She still struggles with guilt. 'In the back of my mind, Mum was always stuck at home and here I was doing what I wanted. I never told them how much I was earning. I liked to bring things down to a level they could relate to.'

Women have other specific issues to contend with. Many organisations are male dominated and many men collude with the belief that women are less competent. Once they reach the top levels, women can find they are unwelcome and this only adds to their insecurities. Men, and the businesses they run, may frame women's achievements as down to positive discrimination. This can often be the case for women of colour, when in fact they have had to show considerably more strength, determination and overcome more obstacles to achieve their success.

While men's insecurities are often located in the office, women feel an added pressure to be good mothers, spouses and social organisers. With increasing expectations at home as well as work, there are more possibilities of being exposed and feeling an impostor, both in one's professional and personal lives. While men are rarely judged on their ability to juggle work and family demands, this continues to be an extra burden on women.

Kathy and her boyfriend subsequently married. Although she still struggles with intimacy, she is determined to make the relationship work. She continues to reduce her hours in the office and her expectations of herself and staff are more reasonable. Jenny, meanwhile, is considering options for returning to work or possibly enrolling in an MA course to enhance her skills. She is determined to find a vocation she loves. William, with insight and understanding, came to acknowledge his achievements and enjoy the fruits of his decisions. He spends more time with his family, finds tremendous joy playing in a band and in close friends. More crucially, he is able to find the compassion for himself that he lacked at work.

Here are tips to help you overcome the impostor syndrome. From the descriptions in this chapter, try to identify if you are struggling with normal self-doubt, or something that needs deeper attention. If what you are dealing with is bearable, try to turn these thoughts to your advantage. Recognise that some self-doubt is not only normal but can also help spur you on to achieve more. Identify areas that you need to improve on. Perhaps you would benefit by having a mentor – someone who can help you gain perspective.

If intense and excruciating feelings do not diminish despite having gained experience in your role, then you need to examine yourself and try the following:

**Keep a curious mindset.** When highjacked by fear and insecurity the mind naturally turns inward and one becomes self-absorbed. Focusing your attention on other people will not only take you out of yourself but also reduce your anxiety and develop your interpersonal skills. You are also likely to discover that other people are equally insecure and frightened of being found out. Knowing how to read this syndrome by recognising defences in colleagues can help you identify how they tick. Next time you see someone in the office avoiding new tasks, overworking or being especially harsh on staff performance, they may well be struggling with the same crippling feelings.

A young executive recounted to me his difficulties with a client who was unapproachable, gave little away and could not grasp how my client was trying to help him. On further discussion, it became apparent that the client was recently promoted, tended to rely on what he was good at and avoided discussing issues outside his knowledge. I suggested focusing on building trust with him by offering plenty of reassurance and avoiding discussing areas outside his comfort zone until a trusting relationship had been established.

**Separating rational from irrational thoughts is vital.** There may indeed be areas where one needs to learn, where weaknesses and limitations need to be acknowledged and addressed.

Irrational thoughts, however, need to be understood. Understanding where they come from will help lessen the intensity of feelings, as will talking to others and sharing your experiences. These tips can help turn panic into reasonable self-doubt.

**Recognise that uncertainty is a reality of working life.** Accept that bad decisions happen and failure is always a possibility. Are you being realistic or too harsh on yourself? Find compassion for yourself and re-evaluate your expectations.

# 3

# Is fear of rejection cramping your style? – or, when people pleasing becomes compulsive

Of my various occupations and sidelines before I began my psychotherapy career, the most exhilarating was a stint as a stand-up on the London comedy circuit in the early 1990s. For all my strenuous efforts at raising the roof, however, the success required to leave the day job behind never materialised. Yet treading the comedic boards taught me one crucially important lesson for life, which is best illustrated by one particularly disastrous night at a leading London comedy venue . . .

*I'm booked on the bill as Naomi Rose at the Banana Cabaret, a popular and friendly venue in Balham. Shragai is a bit of a pronunciation nightmare so I decided to go with a snappier version of me – Naomi Rose. At only five foot two, I also convinced myself that 'Rose' gave me a taller appearance. Recently, my good gigs have more than made up for the bad ones, so I'm feeling confident – so much so that I have invited some close friends along and one of them is even bringing his mother.*

*On arrival at the pub I say a quick hello to my chums and the club's promoters and make my way to the loo. There, staring at the mirror, I rehearse my lines. Firing up my energy and with a smile on my face, I voice aloud my first gag: 'Hi, I'm Naomi. I'm originally from Los Angeles, LA, but now I live in London, L.'*

*I'm suddenly interrupted. A woman enters to use the toilet. I pretend to put on lipstick so as not to appear an odd woman who talks to herself. I wait, she washes her hands, leaves and I continue. 'The hardest thing I ever had to do when moving from LA to London is change my driving habits. The first time I drove in London, I was concentrating on keeping to the left when I saw a pedestrian trying to cross the road on my right. Confused, I didn't know where to look – old American habits kicked in, you know what it's like; I shot him.'*

*I return to the dressing room, peeking at the stage as the comedy begins. The compere is doing a great job. The gags are rolling, the audience, standing or seated at tables, is predictably receptive and laughing at all the right moments. The energy is high; I feel a glow of happiness in my heart and excitement in my belly. Next on is Noel James from Wales. I love his surreal humour – everything about him makes me laugh.*

*'My name is Noel James. That's right, I was an Easter baby,' he says in his delightful Welsh lilt.*

*'I was waiting for Godot the other day. Wouldn't you know it, three came along at the same time.'*

*Noel waltzes through his set; the audience love him. Big applause, then an interval and I'm next. Suddenly, panic strikes me. My confidence is replaced by terror. My legs go numb and my mouth dry. My heart is racing and I feel it pounding, as if about to burst out of my chest.*

*The lights dim and the compere brings the audience to attention. He gets more laughs and warms them up well. But my heart's sudden sprinting session has not stopped.*

*'And now, we have a very funny lady. You may have seen her before. She's been around the circuit for a while now and she always*

*makes me laugh. So, please give a big welcoming round of applause for Naomi Rose!'*

*Walking across the stage to the microphone I immediately sense hostility from the audience. The huge welcoming round of applause I was expecting does not arrive. Instead, a cool polite clap. I feel the spotlight on me and pull the microphone out of its stand with gusto to show I mean business. Before I open my mouth, however, I realise the crowd is not with me, and quickly decide to move my best gags forward.*

*'I live with my best friend Karen. Every night she stays home to knit while I'm out trying desperately to meet a guy. At the end of the year at least she has a fucking jumper to show for it.'*

*I love this gag because it is true and it always works. Not this time. Cold silence . . . 'Keep going, I still have a chance to turn this around. Hit them with your best gag,' I tell myself.*

*'I've tried all kinds of therapies, I've been to homeopaths, osteopaths and even tried a naturopath – no one seemed to help. Eventually, I ended up seeing a psychopath. You may think I'm mad but he solved all my problems – he shot my family.'*

*The room is quiet. There's no denying it – I am 'dying'. The audience's silent coldness turns to boredom, which then turns to chatter. People are talking among themselves. I am being crushed by a massive weight of collective rejection. As I am now being completely ignored, I decide to put everyone, including myself, out of their misery and quietly leave the stage. To add to my humiliation, the next comic, Dylan Moran, goes down a storm.*

Comedy is a risky business. There is good reason why comics are said to 'die' when they can't get the audience to laugh, while other performers are described as merely 'having a bad night.' The silence is excruciating and there is no one to share it with. The burden is yours alone, as is the humiliation and accompanying shame. The extreme highs of my good gigs were almost as difficult to come down from as was coming up from the lows of poor ones. When a room full of people concludes you are bad, it's hard to disagree. It took me days to recover from this particular night but I did crawl back from the experience to perform for a few more years.

And the lesson of this night and my subsequent career? The single most necessary skill to succeed as a stand-up comic, even above talent, is the ability to survive rejection. If you can return to performing after a 'death,' which happens to everyone at some point, you have a chance of success. Comedy taught me that rejection feels terrible but it does not actually kill. More broadly, it showed me that overcoming rejection is crucial to success in any field.

Excessive rejection when I was young prepared me for a career on the comedy circuit. As a child in California, I was not good at much. In high school, I elected to join a folk dancing class to avoid the inevitable 'being the last to be chosen for a sports team' syndrome. Unlike my peers who were good at maths, languages or music, I had no such talents. Although IQ tests deemed me gifted, as a child, I fell to the bottom of every class. My low grades prevented me applying for any college entrance exam. I was rescued by California's community college system which fortunately had the most minimal prerequisites – to be over the age of 18 and breathing. At last, I could meet the requirements. My friends and I later joked that even if you weren't breathing, they would prop you up.

I went on to gain a degree from the University of Southern California, which wiped out my previous failures. I was on my way. Yet those early years of rejection made it a theme close to my heart. Anticipation of rejection kept my expectations low but I learnt to get back on my feet, plough on and any subsequent achievement was a bonus.

Many people have the courage not only to withstand rejection but also grow from it. Creatives, for example, think beyond what is familiar and safe to seek novel solutions, but often their ideas are at first dismissed. The most successful creative thinkers have hardened themselves for disappointment and this is what sets them apart. They know most of their ideas are likely to be trashed and never see the light of day, and yet they persevere, while most of us dare not risk damaging our reputations by being seen as wrong, stupid or inept.

We can be so convinced that others will judge us harshly that we keep good ideas to ourselves. Think about the last time you had an opinion, a question or an idea that you played out in your head and dismissed before you voiced the thought. Had you already concluded you might be ridiculed, rejected or ignored? Did you fear being disliked, humiliated or just being wrong? Think of the times you may have missed an opportunity because you swallowed your words. Start to accumulate evidence of how fear of rejection has undermined you professionally. Staring at the hard facts might motivate you to examine what lies behind your fears.

It is, in the main, not others who judge us harshly but ourselves. Obsessing that our ideas are 'wrong' or 'no good', we believe others share that opinion. We project our negative thoughts on to others as if they do not have minds of their own. Without exposing our ideas to the light of day where they can be explored and discussed, we miss an opportunity to see the value we bring and hear what other people actually think. Furthermore, we risk undermining our careers if we become out of touch with our opinions, ambitions and direction.

Social media have much to answer for in this regard. The obsession to gain 'likes' in order to boost one's self-esteem has grown out of proportion to the extent that one's internal gauge is lost. Developing professionally, learning new skills and fulfilling one's ambitions are somehow ranked below the accumulation of 'likes'. It is as if one's experience is not real unless it is shared and applauded on social media. Being liked – above all else – becomes the goal rather than a professional or personal achievement.

Certainly, rejection feels excruciating and you might conclude that all attempts to avoid it are reasonable. After all, we are social animals and crave to connect. Threats of exclusion make us panic. We can instinctively go against our best instincts, submit to others' opinions and even abandon our ambitions to fit in and belong. We depend on our families, friends, our workplace and other organisations – whether they be football clubs, religious or other social groups – to provide us with a sense of identity, belonging and security. Such institutions also offer comfort in hard times, companionship, hope against hopelessness and support in grief. In turn, we offer our loyalty. Our dependency leaves us reluctant to disagree, to go against the grain and to speak out about wrongs. When our membership of these groups is threatened, we fear for our identity and well-being, and our instincts are to go to extreme measures to be accepted back into the fold.

So while avoiding rejection is understandable, it is when you experience an extreme compulsion to make others feel better to the detriment of yourself that alarm bells should ring. Compulsive 'people pleasers' are good examples – they will go to inordinate lengths to be liked. Their dependent personality means their need for security subsumes their ambitions and drives, and the image they display reflects how they imagine others would like them to be rather than who they actually are. At work, they tend to be long-standing, competent employees, good team players and sensitive to others' needs. They are the followers to the leaders, the audience to the creatives and the listening ear to the troubled colleague. They rarely engage in disputes with colleagues and in many ways are the bread-and-butter stalwarts of organisations. However, their emotional antennae tend to be directed more outward than inward. Tuning into other people leaves them less aware of their own internal landscape. They suppress their emotions and opinions, lose sight of their direction and, most worryingly, disconnect from themselves. While colleagues benefit from their generosity, they themselves are the ultimate losers, neither fulfilling their potential nor gaining the satisfaction of a career pursued to its maximum. Ignoring their own thoughts, opinions and ideas, they become dependent on bosses and colleagues to make decisions and even think for them. And although companies gain from their steadfast, co-operative effort, they nevertheless miss out on their unique talents. Such is how the cycle of pleasing and dependency gains momentum. When thoughts are not vocalised, they are not energised and change and development are stunted.

Motivation is crucial to escape this cycle. When the compulsion to please clashes with one's ambitions, internal conflict arises. While such tension is uncomfortable, it can fuel the motivation necessary for change. Both personal and professional growth can be achieved if one is willing to face and work through these conflicts and confusions.

This was the case for a 39-year-old single man, David, who worked in publishing. His charm and wit created a perfect cover for his deeper insecurities but they were not far from the surface.

A promotion had forced him to confront his conflict between wanting to please and to succeed. Pleasing people had been a lifelong survival strategy against the threat of rejection. This stood him in good stead in early work roles but when promoted to a leadership position his fear of rejection undermined his capacity to take tough decisions and have difficult conversations.

I wanted to know more. 'Can you explain how your fears undermine your performance at work?'

'It's inhibiting because the decisions you make are layered in lots of considerations about how the other person might feel, or react, or how they might be motivated to speak against you, and how they might recruit others against you,' he said. 'You compensate by masking your own intent so as not to offend them or diluting what you're going to say. That means you're less efficient, less productive.

'Even if there's a fraction of a chance they might be

offended, I hold back. You don't want to risk people being offended because they may walk away or get others to walk away, too. If you're preoccupied with making sure the person doesn't dislike you then you're not being honest. So, you feel crappy about yourself and they feel like they're not getting the direct message that you should be conveying.'

I was concerned that his hyper-vigilant state of mind left him constantly anticipating the next threat. I told him: 'Staying on high alert often puts you on the brink of an anxiety attack and your irrational worries about others means you betray yourself.'

'If you take people on then you're creating enemies,' he responded. 'You work out a way to avoid doing this by trying to make other people feel good about themselves. At the same time, you suppress your own personality. Everything is calculated – it's a performance and that's what's exhausting because you're creating an image that's designed to make sure you're not rejected.'

I explained to him that his new, more senior position did not help him because he still believed others – whether underlings, colleagues or clients – held sway because they had the power to reject him. As a result, his confidence diminished and he pushed himself to work harder to demonstrate his worth but the long hours were leading to burnout. He was likely to misread situations, seeing threats where none existed, or become so preoccupied that an actual threat was missed.

'I've not taken something seriously when I should have done,' he admitted, 'or I've been ready for a battle when I've just misread the signs.'

The concern he showed for others was actually a strategy to distance himself from deeper emotional traumas from his early life. Many wrongly assume that trauma is limited to extreme experiences, such as sexual abuse, terrorism or war. Trauma is in fact an emotional and physical response to any unbearable event. The mind rushes to protect the individual from overwhelming feelings, such as grief, helplessness or rage, by numbing these emotions. But traces of such experiences remain in our memories, emotions, unconscious and even our bodies, and have a lasting effect on how we think, relate to others, regulate our emotions and process our experiences. This includes how we interpret events and react in the workplace.

Often, ordinary work disappointments can ignite early traumatic experiences and this was the case for David. He was an adored son born after his mother had lost two children, one to a miscarriage and one stillborn. Understandably, he was the centre of his mother's world. We all need to believe we have such a place in our mother's heart when we are small and dependent but in time we learn the harsh truth that the wider world may not universally hold us in such high regard.

In David's case, the shock that he was not similarly adored by others came when, aged 11, he entered secondary school and discovered he was not special, but ordinary. The blow made him withdrawn and as a result he was teased by other children. He secretly wished his mother would recognise his withdrawn behaviour as a plea for help. Instead, she interpreted his sulks as criticism of her.

'When I withdrew, she didn't know how to cope. I lost my

energy and all of the things she most worshipped in me, which were being smart and funny – they vanished and were replaced by "I don't know what to do"."

In his late teens David discovered that by making others feel good about themselves he could escape the isolation and rejection he experienced. He brought these strategies into his professional life as protection from the risk of rejection he imagined always loomed. Thus, while people pleasing helped him progress at work, unconsciously it was also keeping his early traumatic feelings at bay. Yet after his promotion his inner conflict grew. I pointed out to him that while a part of him recognised he was undermining his ability to lead, another feared giving up the strategy that had helped him succeed and protected him from overwhelming emotions from childhood.

These insights have helped him separate the past from the present and allowed him to make small but significant changes. Recognising that many situations he perceived as threats were located in his internal world and early life, rather than in the workplace, was the beginning. He now challenges his thoughts rather than acting on them, asking himself if a situation is a real threat or a perceived one. He is more willing to risk voicing his opinions with clients and staff, although he monitors carefully what might be a high risk compared with a low one. Gradually, he is building the emotional muscle necessary for tolerating uncomfortable situations.

Questioning and reflecting on one's thoughts and perceptions is the crucial first step. But when obsessive thoughts dominate, achieving a new mindset can be extremely difficult.

Talking with someone – a confidant or a professional – can help turn a self-defeating monologue into a creative dialogue. Such conversations plant in people's minds fresh understandings and perspectives, and this can be integrated with previous experiences to arrive at a more positive mindset.

The source of David's fears of rejection was secondary school but for others it is often in the first months or early years when dependency on a caregiver is all encompassing. Our 'attachment' relationship to our mothers or other caregivers sets a template for how we relate to others throughout our lives – whether closeness feels comforting or threatening and how willing we are to trust, collaborate and empathise.

Take a moment to consider your comfort zone at work. Do you often perceive a situation as dangerous when it is not? Do you tend to keep a distance from colleagues, or do you prefer to work closely with others? Do you crave validation? How easily do you trust others?

Awareness of your attachment relationships is the best place to start. In his seminal work on attachment in the 1950s, British psychoanalyst John Bowlby recognised that the infant is motivated as much by need for comfort and security as by physical needs. The attachment figure, usually the mother, becomes a secure base from which the baby can explore the world. The need for comfort and security never ceases but those who experienced a secure base in early life are more likely to feel confident that others will respond to them with the same care. They are more likely to feel competent, worthwhile and loveable.

'Attachment requires much more than physical care and

protection,' Peter Fonagy, the leading child psychoanalyst and world-renowned specialist in attachment disorders, explained to me. 'It becomes about supporting the development of the human mind – to be able to describe one's inner experience, to be able to anticipate what others feel and think and to have social collaboration – these things are dependent on attachment relationships.

'When a child feels secure, what we really mean by that is that they have a capacity to regulate their own feelings to be able to interact well with peers, to be able to understand others well, to be able to think about and be empathetic and considerate with those around them, at the same time as being sufficiently confident about their inner experience. To know their own mind. That's secure attachment.'

However, where parents or caretakers have been extremely neglectful, chaotic or anxious, especially in the first two years of life, individuals may be left with psychological scars as well as lasting imprints in their brains and nervous systems affecting the mechanisms responsible for impulse control, regulation of feelings and connection with others.

People with insecure attachments are more likely to suffer anxieties of being rejected and criticised or have exaggerated worries of being forgotten or unacknowledged. In the workplace, these dysfunctional attachment patterns can manifest in the following ways: at one extreme, persistently seeking approval from others, becoming too clingy or needy, or overcompensating by making themselves indispensable. At the other extreme, they become too distant and self-reliant, isolating themselves because closeness feels intolerable. Believing others are out to harm them, they find it difficult to collaborate. Although they long for connections, they never trust the relationships they make. Ordinary work disappointments, such as being ignored or overlooked for a promotion, can sometimes feel life threatening when early attachment disorders and feelings of abandonment and rejection are reignited, as the case below illustrates.

Max is a tall, well-mannered man in his thirties with a gentle tone who has his own marketing consultancy. Not long into our work, he revealed how his deep longing to be liked by clients was putting his business at risk because transactional interactions felt intensely personal. His fear of rejection stemmed from a dysfunctional attachment relationship with his mother, which resulted in him feeling unloveable and worthless. She was an academic, dedicated to her career, but cold and dispassionate in nature. Although his parents provided a physically and intellectually secure environment, they were not able to tune into his emotional needs for comfort.

To gain his mother's attention, Max became the bridge builder in the family, the peaceful and amicable one, to a disproportionate degree. From an early age he concluded that the best way to get his mother to respond to him was to do chores around the house and not be difficult. Because she lacked a capacity to tune into his needs, he focused his attention on her. This is where he learnt to attend to others in order to connect.

In business, this translated into caring for the people he depended on – his clients and colleagues. His fear of rejection was so intense that he struggled to approach potential clients. He describes how his underlying neediness interfered with his capacity to offer a professional service: 'I have a level of professional competence which people want to buy but I've also got a capacity to shoot myself in the foot with clients because I have a tendency to try to second guess them out of a desire for their validation.

'I'm generally quite good at judgement and reading a room and understanding what's needed but then I can often allow myself to get in the way of all that good stuff by worrying whether I'm liked or not. What is essentially a transactional relationship – where someone is paying for my expertise – gets muddied by a neediness that gets in the way of me being able to give good judgement, advice and strategic perspective, which is ultimately what they're paying for.

'It's really a proxy for "Am I lovable?" and if not, "Could I be rejected and if so, what catastrophic consequences might follow from that?" The worst that can happen is that a client might not renew my contract. It's not as if the world will end, and yet it feels like it could.

'I can find myself feeling paralysed in an infantile way where I find it quite difficult to function. In that moment I catastrophise – "Will I be rejected?" That anxiety – fear of rejection – is completely incompatible with what it is to deliver a good professional service to a client.'

'What you refer to as "validation from clients",' I said, 'is a proxy for the emotional comfort you craved from your mother.' From his expression it was clear I had touched a nerve.

He continued: 'All through my school years I was good at not exposing my mum and dad to any of my difficult feelings, lest it might hurt them. Some of the things that have crippled me most in life is when I have not shared. What happens is I don't open up emotionally and I catastrophise. On one level, I felt loved. I had parents who put food on the table and gave me good intellectual challenges, who did love me. But the love they gave didn't fill a need in a way that I play out in a professional context.'

However irrational, the mind revisits unresolved events from the past in order to seek resolution.

I suggested to him: 'I think you are attempting to gain in your business the emotional comfort you missed as a child.' Constantly anticipating rejection while craving 'validation' trapped him in a cycle of needing but not achieving the security he craved.

To resolve these issues he first had to face the harsh truth that seeking emotional comfort through transactional relationships at work was likely to fail. Separating his internal and historic needs from his desire to succeed in his business was the next step. Work is about networking, promoting oneself, achieving results and making money. Personal relationships, on the other hand, are about emotional connections, security, feeling that you matter to the other person and will not be forgotten. These are deeply human needs we all possess. The confusion arises when we attempt to meet these needs in the workplace. Max also had to focus on his 'healthy' and mature side, which is ambitious, intelligent, experienced and creative. Reminding himself of his stronger traits would help quieten his more irrational side.

Max has progressed in many ways. He catastrophises less and although he has worries, they are realistic. He is less driven by his internal motivation to please others and more focused on what is needed to get the job done. Rather than forgetting or belittling his accomplishments, he recognises and builds on his successes, and relies less on others for validation of his worth.

Changing behaviour is challenging on many fronts. Although people can insist they want to change, when they repeat the same unwanted behaviour it exposes that a larger, perhaps unconscious part of them is too frightened or unwilling to do so. What they often fear is facing repressed feelings or the resulting confusion. If the prospect of conflict or opposing a popular view leaves one feeling extremely anxious, resorting to survival strategies such as people pleasing relieves the discomfort. Reverting to type becomes a mood stabiliser – it makes one feel better.

If you find yourself people pleasing to an extent that overrides your professional ambitions or you hold back your ideas for fear of how they might be received, you should consider the cost to your creative potential and career advancement. You may have a compulsive need to please people if you:

- Find yourself agreeing to an extent that you have lost your voice.
- Rely on others to make decisions.
- No longer have strong opinions but rather 'go with the flow.'
- Have not advanced in your career for many years despite being well liked by colleagues and management.
- Are better at tuning into others' needs rather than your own.

Next, identify your fears of rejection. For example, do you fear:

- Being disliked?
- Being excluded or forgotten?
- A potential retaliation from colleagues?
- Losing the security and safety that the workplace provides?

Facing your fears is the first step to challenging them. Are they realistic, or are you reacting to historic hurts and injuries? If your fears are more historic than current, recognise that they are no longer applicable to the workplace.

Even when we make progress, where we find ourselves in our minds will always feel like the new normal and this can be confusing when attempting to measure one's psychological growth. Remind yourself where you began as opposed to where you have arrived. Development is not straightforward. Your fears can never be entirely banished, but they need not control you. There will be regressions but this does not mean that you have not advanced.

Remember that your fears and anxieties, no matter how you wish to be free of them, also make you who you are. These feelings, even though you might regret them, are an important part of your life experience and help tell your story. And recognising them helps you to change that story.

# 4

# Overachievement has its limits – or, the unintended costs of success

Kerry Sulkowicz, a colleague and friend, recalls his father saying to him at the age of eight: 'You can do anything you like – as long as you go to medical school first.' From then, he never felt he had a choice in the matter. He has since become a psychiatrist, psychoanalyst and adviser to some of the world's top business leaders.

Kerry was the only child of Jewish Polish parents who survived Nazi concentration camps while many of their relatives perished. After the Second World War, they made their home far away in Texas. From an early age, Kerry had internalised his parents' psychological damage, together with the belief that he could not let them down after what they had endured.

'That heightened my belief of not wanting to hurt them or disappoint them by not living up to this idea of going to medical school,' he told me from his home in New York.

Being a doctor, his father believed, would provide him with a readily transferable skill should there come another time when Jews had to flee. Such is the understandable mentality of refugees who know that sometimes all you can take with you is what you have learnt. Survivor guilt was another motivating factor for Kerry – he felt he needed to make up for the opportunities that were denied to his parents and this pushed him to strive harder.

'You're never perfect but you can always strive for the highest level of achievement and anything less was somehow a personal failure. It was a crazy idea but that has driven me.'

He excelled academically at school, as a student at Harvard and later in medical school at the University of Texas. He took any opportunity to enhance his professional training after deciding to become a psychiatrist and psychoanalyst.

From an early age he was also drawn to leadership roles, beginning with the editorship of his high school newspaper and captain of its fencing team. Later in life, he became founder and managing principal of the Boswell Group, which advises business chiefs and other senior leaders, chair of Physicians for Human Rights and President-elect of the American Psychoanalytic Association.

'One of the factors is that because my parents were so damaged, I had to take care of them and I was kind of a leader in my own home when I was a little kid,' he explained. 'Another thing about being a leader that was largely unconscious until I figured it out, was that being a leader lessened my feelings of dependency. I would rather people depend on me than me having to be dependent on them.'

Only after he graduated from medical school did he realise that he did not like looking after sick people after all and was ill-suited to being anything medically other than a psychiatrist. Kerry's parents never fully understood his roles as a psychoanalyst or adviser to leaders. When he was once interviewed by the

*Wall Street Journal* he sent a copy of the article to his mother, thinking she would be thrilled to see her son's name in a prestigious national newspaper. It so happened that the newspaper's style was not to use the title of 'Dr,' just Mr or Ms instead, so he was quoted as 'Mr Sulkowicz.' When he had no response from her for more than a week, he telephoned.

'I thought you'd be thrilled to see my name in the *WSJ*,' he told her.

His mother replied with alarm in her voice: 'Kerry, I was so upset after reading that article because they called you "Mr". Does that mean you're no longer a doctor?'

Most of us aspire to achieve, which is healthy and beneficial for ourselves and society. There is nothing wrong with wanting to be the best one can, to earn well and gain recognition and admiration from peers and family. Kerry, thanks to his own personal development, training and experience, is fully aware of his drive to achieve but for the more neurotic extreme overachiever, unrealistically high expectations mean perspective is lost to the extent of not only putting one's physical and mental health at risk but also potentially damaging a business.

The psychological trait of extreme overachieving came to the fore in the 1980s, a time of free-market politics, financial deregulation, buccaneering entrepreneurs and ruthless investment banks and financial traders. The spirit of the times was memorably captured in films such as *Wall Street*, which coined the 'greed is good' slogan, and books such as Tom Wolfe's *The Bonfire of the Vanities*, with its millionaire 'masters of the universe' bond traders.

There is no doubt that overachievers are capable of extraordinary accomplishments and little wonder they are much sought after by many companies. In fact, some organisations, particularly in the banking, finance and legal sectors, have been known to intentionally recruit ambitious overachievers, creating cultures that further exploit and manipulate their character. Working for the most prestigious organisations makes overachievers feel they are the best by association. It eventually becomes clear to them, however, that there is a price to be paid.

Professor Laura Empson of Cass Business School, and author of *Leading Professionals: Power, Politics, and Prima Donnas*, told me that many insecure overachievers soon discover that the rigorous up-or-out policy that such organisations employ, which demands one excels or be fired, exacerbates their insecurity. Professor Empson says such cultural practices also exist in more subtle ways. Companies that offer mental health initiatives or on-site gyms, for example, create an illusion of being a benign organisation that supposedly looks after its employees but the demands of the job often make it difficult to use these facilities. The onus is put on the individual while the company absolves itself of responsibility.

'It's like saying we've got a counsellor, why aren't you happier? If the work is constructed in such a way that you haven't the time or energy to go to the gym or feel it's all right to see the counsellor, then it becomes your fault.'

Convinced they are underperforming in comparison with others who are visibly setting relentlessly high standards of achievement, overachievers work harder. With everybody doing this, the standard can only get higher and higher.

'You only need a few people in an organisation to be setting the bar for what is an appropriate standard of achievement, for everyone else to feel inadequate,' she adds.

The rewards for overworking, however, can be substantial, both for individuals and the companies they work for. Overachievers come to depend on their financial earnings and the lifestyle it brings. High mortgage payments, lavish holidays and, for many, private school fees are other marks of their success that add to the pressure. Complacency is never an option – in their minds it leads to decline in performance and eventually to termination. It is precisely because their success is tied to their excessive work habits that they are reluctant to change. But there is more – their habits are also tied to deeper psychological structures, which I will explore later in this chapter.

Like many psychological traits I discuss in this book, overachieving runs along a continuum of healthy and productive at one end towards destructive at the other. Although where one is on this continuum is influenced by external factors such as one's profession, the employer and changing societal norms, I believe it is the individual's internal drives that can send them over the tipping point towards the harmful end. While they may not need more money nor to work so hard, they cannot stop. It is these people I will refer to as neurotic overachievers.

Although the compulsion to achieve is common and easy to recognise in investment banking and other elite organisations, it also exists elsewhere. Indeed, anyone who uses achievement to solve a psychological problem to the extent that it harms them, people close to them or their business, is a neurotic overachiever. Fear of failure is an underlying driving force. Failure implies weakness, a trait they despise and deny in themselves. They believe others would also find their weakness undesirable – who would be interested in a failure? Furthermore, any setback is not simply a failure but has the potential to wipe out all previous achievements.

One overachiever told me how he remembered throwing a silver medal away because his high school rowing team did not win the gold. 'We always wanted to come first and anything less was essentially last. If we won a silver or bronze we would dispose of those medals – throw them in the water because it wasn't gold. If you didn't win the race, then you lost the race. Why would you be given a medal for a race you didn't win?' He spoke as if the event happened yesterday rather than 40 years ago.

His compulsion to always be first carried him through many successful years in finance – though he did not restrict it to the office. Decades later, he still had to be the first off the train when commuting to work.

He had a sister with mental health problems, which meant that his parents were often preoccupied by her during their childhood. From a young age, however, he learnt that winning gained his parents' attention. And then when he discovered that 'being the best' not only won parental pride but also social status, he never let himself rest.

Sadly, overachievers are unable to process their successes in a way that provides a lasting sense of accomplishment or satisfaction from their work. Quite the contrary, they can never relax because it makes them feel guilty. Although they allow themselves a thrill from a financial coup or successful deal, this is short-lived because each triumph is quickly discarded. Consequently, they are continuously raising the bar and escalating the cycle of achieving a 'win', followed by an inevitable mood crash and then needing to excel further to rejuvenate their spirits.

As Melissa, a 39-year-old overachiever and head of a successful business, told me: 'Once [an accomplishment] is achieved, it's almost immediately forgotten. The focus has to be solely on the next goal, which needs to be higher. I always looked at everything like a ladder – you always need to be moving up to the next rung. It's about pushing and striving to always better yourself.'

Melissa's story is a striking illustration of the motivations for, and pitfalls, of overachievement. Her fierce determination to push beyond her body's capabilities began at the age of ten with competitive gymnastics, a sport that required much dedication and goal planning. It was here that she cultivated a 'no pain, no gain' philosophy.

'I had an aversion to weakness and excuses, and lack of determination,' she recalled. 'When people couldn't handle things I thought of it as giving up – and giving up for me was never an option.'

Exploring further back, she told me that when she was only six months old, her parents separated bitterly and, much against her mother's wishes, Melissa lived with her father. For the next three years she had no contact with her mother until a legal judgement ensured she was returned to her. This early trauma left her with a fear of separation and drilled into her the need to be self-sufficient to be secure.

Her early successes boosted her self-esteem, but more importantly they induced pride and respect from her mother, which she desperately craved. She had always admired her mother's career success and, for Melissa, respect was another currency of love. This, combined with her talent for sport and ability to excel academically, produced her determination to succeed, to be admired and respected so as not to be forgotten or abandoned.

'Of course, wrapped in that is wanting to please my mother and make her proud of me. She was my role model and I respected her so much. I wanted that in return – I wanted her to respect me and be proud of me. She was a critical person but also complimentary.'

Another contributing factor was her mother's narcissism – she prioritised appearance above all else but Melissa maintained that she did not have her mother's looks and so worked hard to gain the attention she longed for through her achievements. I was struck by the fact that her actual beauty did little to convince her that she need not overcompensate with hard work – such is the power of the mind.

'I knew I was not the movie-star beauty my mother was and she would point that out. I decided where I could shine was in school and in sports, and I carried that forward into work.'

Melissa's mother told her she would be satisfied if she gave any endeavour her all. She repeatedly said: 'Any goal is possible as long as you are willing to work hard enough to achieve it.'

I suggested to Melissa that she had come to believe that if she did not achieve her goal, it was as if she was a failure herself.

She agreed. 'I internalised that until I felt a failure . . . I must not have done enough. That led to a feeling of not being enough. This philosophy was working in the background throughout my life.'

After attending Harvard Law School, she worked at a prestigious law firm. Adrenaline helped her maintain the long hours, as did 'pushing through the fatigue' that she learnt from gymnastics. Her predilection for hard work was reinforced by the culture and ethos of the law firm. She explained: 'You're the select few – and you're supposed to be tougher mentally than the rest and be able to overcome physical and mental exhaustion.'

Following two years at the law firm, she decided she needed more of a challenge. She walked away from the financial rewards and purchased a struggling business. The challenge enabled her to utilise a broader set of skills and the thrill of making something work that someone else could not seemed irresistible. On reflection, she realised that the smartest move would have been to abandon the business after a year but she was not prepared to have a failure on her hands.

'I was determined to turn it around . . . I eventually did, but it almost killed me. I was working 18 hours or more. Sometimes I slept two hours and there were times I worked through on to the next day and on to the next night. I didn't take a vacation for years. I was tired but figured, that's the price you pay. I knew something was wrong when I had so much energy that

I didn't need to sleep more than a few hours. In the beginning, I thought this was great because I could work even more, instead of thinking "What in the world is wrong with me?"'

Her symptoms worsened to the point that she could no longer ignore the problem. 'I had muscle wasting, my hair was falling out and my heart was racing like crazy, among many other symptoms. It turned out that I had an autoimmune disease called Graves' disease, which ultimately led to the discovery of a tumour.'

Four years on, after surprising doctors with her recovery, her perspective had shifted. 'Now I see the light and the idea of making money and not working hard seems ideal. But it didn't then. A sense of achievement was tied to hard work. If I didn't have to work hard, the achievement was less meaningful. My health problems taught me that I am enough without any achievements. I had to learn how to feel proud and good about myself even if I never achieved anything else in my entire life.'

Melissa is not alone. Many neurotic overachievers only take stock once they become seriously ill. Burnout is common. Such individuals long for the day they can stop but sadly it rarely arrives. Many have spent their entire professional lives focusing on clients' demands to the extent they lose touch with their own needs, longings and direction.

The question remains: how are these overachievers able to sustain the long and gruelling hours while ignoring the body's need for sleep, its prompts of pain and illness? One explanation is the mind's capacity to push aside unwanted feelings through complex and often unconscious defensive strategies that were described in chapter one. Reaction formation

– turning an unacceptable trait into its opposite – is one defence mechanism employed so as not to face parts of themselves they despise or fear. Behind their drive is an opposite desire – a deep longing to shed responsibility and relax. Terrified of being seen as lazy or feeble, however, they overcompensate by pushing themselves harder to an extent unimaginable to most people. Subconsciously they wish they could stop but fear being exposed as a slacker or not up to the job.

Splitting, or all-or-nothing thinking, is another defence they lean on. Anything other than the best is considered a failure and outcomes are reduced to a zero-sum game – there are no grey areas: a gold medal is a win and a silver medal is thrown in the river. This attitude explains why any setback can obliterate all previous accomplishments and why reducing work, even by as little as 5 per cent, can leave them believing they are becoming complacent and not trying hard enough. Ultimately they fear they will underperform and be fired.

Neurotic overachievers also deny how their compulsion harms themselves or those close to them. They fail to see they need not work so hard and that their unrealistically high expectations are putting undue pressure on others. They are blind to how they irritate colleagues and underlings alike with their perfectionistic tendencies and frantic energy.

Like Melissa, many neurotic overachievers come to rely on the 'hit' from a success to regulate their mood and lift them from a crash. The adrenaline rush provides much-needed energy to move on to the next project. The cycle escalates and can become addictive when higher aims are created in order to achieve the same 'hit.' But the higher they go, the more there is to accomplish and the risk of failure multiplies. The need to be the best and on top rarely ceases, even outside the bounds of work.

It is when 'winning' becomes the sole solution to problems that difficulties arise and this is what separates normal achievers from neurotic ones. Although financial gains may solve practical problems, achieving in and of itself cannot repair unconscious conflicts, interpersonal relationships or help one learn to cope with strong feelings. As mentioned in previous chapters, traumatic experiences in early life can leave individuals struggling to regulate their mood. Feeling dreadful as a result of failing, for example, is terrifying if one lacks the ability to overcome this strong emotion. When achieving becomes their sole strategy for easing or regulating such feelings, neurotic overachievers never learn how to tolerate them.

It is commonly believed that overachievers had parents who were overachievers themselves and had high expectations for them, causing their offspring to believe that gaining love and acceptance is intertwined with achievement. While some people I have known fit this description, it is not always the case – individuals are more complex and their backgrounds more diverse. From what I have witnessed over the years, many neurotic overachievers discovered at an early age that accomplishment solved a problem for them – whether it be to gain parental love, protect themselves from harm or distance themselves from a deprived or damaged background. The stories I've come across have been varied but the determination to succeed and avoid failure is the same.

Undoubtedly these people experience extreme stress and

feel under threat. Some imagine that if they have a setback they will be total failures, lose their competitive edge and possibly their jobs. But the question to ask is whether they are reacting to an internal or external threat, and if their reactions are rational or irrational. While external threats clearly exist, the deep compulsion to achieve even to the detriment of one's health or personal relationships is often a reaction to internal ones, such as fear of weakness, inadequacy or insecurity. The compulsion to win can also be understood as a strategy for keeping earlier traumatic experiences at a distance. For overachievers, a failure, or even a setback, risks reigniting past traumas and repressed feelings.

When the body's threat-response system kicks in it releases cortisol – the hormone that fuels the body's fight-or-flight instincts – and adrenaline, which together focus the individual's attention. They both increase heart rate and blood pressure, which results in a surge of energy and mental concentration, thereby distracting the person from the sensation of pain. This explains how individuals become out of touch with cues for rest, sleep and pain, which puts them at further risk of illness and burnout. For instance, take high-flying women who insist on always wearing uncomfortable and damaging high-heeled shoes at work to lift their professional appearance in every respect. One young banker told me she ignored medical advice to switch shoes when suffering early stages of Morton's neuroma, a condition where foot nerve damage causes severe pain. As a result, she suffered irreparable harm to her feet and can now wear only trainers. I was told of another high-achieving pregnant woman who was on a conference call while in labour.

Being able to tell such a tale, I was informed, was a badge of honour.

Many individuals find they cannot sustain the long and gruelling hours for more than six to ten years. Eventually, physical exhaustion overcomes them or damage done to their personal relationships lead to family break-ups. More worrying is that depression and other serious mental health problems can erupt. The mind and body work in unison to push unwanted thoughts and emotions out of awareness and into our bodies in the form of muscular tensions. For overachievers, this helps focus attention on their work, but while these tensions are locked in their bodies they cannot be thought about and dealt with. Instead, they eventually emerge as physical ailments.

Alexandra Michel, a business and leadership consultant and adjunct professor at the University of Pennsylvania Graduate School of Education, carried out research at two US investment banks for more than a decade, beginning in the early 2000s. Her focus was on working practices, the effects on bankers' health and the organisational consequences. She found that for their first three years, young bankers worked excessively long hours, neglecting their bodies and ignoring need for sleep and signs of illness but were nevertheless able to excel. From year four onward, however, many began to suffer mental and physical problems, the former including slipping into addictive behaviour, such as eating disorders, or distractions such as pornography. Their performance and creativity also suffered, as did their capacity to empathise. By year six, about 40 per cent at last began paying attention to their bodies and modifying their work behaviour and their performance levels recovered as a result. The remaining 60 per cent, however, continued on their self-destructive paths to more illness and breakdowns.

There are further problems when neurotic overachievers advance to leadership positions. They often bring their perfectionistic traits with them, treating their staff in the same manner they treat themselves, believing everyone should be just as driven and holding them to the same high standards. They put their staff in a bind, however, by expecting them to work as hard yet are reluctant to hand over responsibility. Their unwanted weakness is projected onto colleagues and underlings, while they believe that they alone are capable of maintaining excellence. They blame the 'incompetence' of their staff for anything that falls short of their expectations rather than their failure to delegate. Their exaggerated sense of responsibility leaves them feeling burdened, but asking for help would be a sign of weakness.

Another problem emerges when such a leader is seen to be putting his or her own advancement or interests ahead of their staff. Such a leader is unlikely to convince his people to follow loyally. More dangerous is when the overachiever's personal agenda undermines the aims or long-term health of the business. The past quarter of a century has seen too many chief executives, for instance, who, motivated by lucrative incentive pay schemes, focused on short-term increases in their company's share price rather than the best long-term strategy. Boosting the next set of profits always trumped necessary long-term investment in the business. The immediate gratification, which reflects well on them, is the only type of success they recognise.

The determination to be top dog at work also extends to being seen as the best spouse. Divorce for these individuals is often not an option because it implies failure. But they lack the emotional intelligence to resolve tensions in the relationship and, as a result, become locked in a bad marriage. They rationalise their overworking as being 'for the good of the family' and place themselves firmly 'in the right' and their spouses 'in the wrong.' As marital tensions grow, they retreat further into work, where they believe they are treated more fairly. Respect and admiration from colleagues are used to reinforce their 'rightness.' It takes emotional maturity to acknowledge one's part in domestic tensions and disputes but in this regard they underachieve woefully. Instead, they handle family frictions in the same way as corporate problems.

Such was the case for Andrew, a 35-year-old entrepreneur, who initially came to me for help regarding his business. I should explain that my consulting room is the front room of my home, conveniently separated from the rest of the ground-floor flat by a reception area. One has a glimpse of this area before entering my consulting room. Andrew's first visit was on a day when the reception area was untidier than usual – bicycles parked messily against the stair banisters, tennis rackets not put back after a recent game – and his appearance, tall and immaculate in an expensive suit and tie, only heightened my self-consciousness about it.

He spoke quickly and convincingly so as not to allow a gap

in the conversation – lest anything negative be said. As I listened, his overachieving personality soon became clear. 'It's a yearning to get out there and beat a personal record that I've set,' he explained. 'I want to better myself, improve myself and push myself. If I don't do my best, I feel disappointed. If I do, I know I'm improving. To have a tangible thing, where I can see improvement month after month – other things in my life are harder to control.'

One of those 'other things', it emerged, was that his character trait was causing problems in his marriage. For him, and others like him, a project that he can control feels more manageable than the complexity and unpredictability of intimacy.

His early determination to succeed was motivated by a craving for admiration. He explained that he was the eldest and favoured child in his modest working-class family, adored by parents and grandparents alike. From an early age, the sense of being adored motivated him until it became addictive. While he worked hard to maintain his special position in the family, he never learnt how to cope with rejection, criticism or indeed any unpleasant feeling.

While his parents created a secure 'attachment' in his early years, it was not enough to ease his need to excel. His parents' caring attention could not be repeated later in life. Such a warm, loving and secure base can leave one unprepared for a world that can be harsh and unfair. Andrew's defence against this was to double down on his drive to succeed and keep rejection and criticism at bay.

One memory of returning from a school trip to a sports

centre at the age of six is telling. 'On the way back, I had this sense of I just need to do my homework. Everyone else was laughing – but I knew I had to do my homework.'

He discovered that by working hard he would always be at the top of his game, never let his parents down and, in the process, avoid bad feelings altogether. 'I'm also praised by family for being supportive and loving, gentle towards them,' he explained. 'I wanted to strive for perfection. It means I can never let my guard down and expose myself to criticism.'

The drive to do his absolute best continued throughout a successful education and into his well-rewarded professional life. Crucially for him, he continued to feel 'special' and admired. There were, however, chinks in the armour, such as his chronic anxiety. He dealt with it by gaining success after success in business. While each one helped lessen his anxiety, there would be the inevitable downward mood swing afterwards and then the ensuing need to raise his game again to regain equilibrium – a continual raising of the bar, which in turn fed another cycle of anxiety.

He told me: 'I get the inevitable endorphins when I meet the goal, then the inevitable crash afterwards.'

His work life, like any, was not without frustrations and personal tensions. In order to maintain his admirable image, however, he would need to repress his frustrations and anger. Yet these negative feelings had to be expressed somewhere – so where?

In our later conversations, it became clear that his wife took the brunt of them. He found himself frequently irritated by what he perceived as an onslaught of criticism from her.

His resentment was expressed either verbally or by distancing himself and both reactions infuriated her.

I suggested that he was frustrated that she did not respond to him with the same admiration lavished on him by colleagues and clients.

'Somewhere you believe she should be even more understanding than colleagues and are shocked that she could be harsh,' I said. 'You seem to interpret the respect you get from others as evidence that the fault in the relationship lies with her.'

There were further problems. The business was growing and this meant increased complexity and the realisation that he would not be able to sustain his level of involvement in every aspect of it. Following a period of executive coaching, he admitted that the time for change had come. His fear of failure and compulsive work habits were putting both his business and marriage at risk.

This change understandably proved difficult. The idea of reducing work, even a little, made him anxious. Anything other than doing his best was 'lazy'; his work ethic gave him a sense of control and financial success had resulted. But the biggest obstacle was more deep rooted. His drive and ambition shielded him from negative feelings and criticism.

With these insights his motivation to change has increased and he has been able to make significant changes in order for his business to expand. He is able to relinquish control over aspects of it and has reduced his late-night hours. He is delegating more and tolerating the anxiety of unfinished tasks. He also recognises that his future well-being depends on having a strong partnership with his wife.

Unlike others, Andrew was fortunate – matters had not reached the point of marital breakdown, serious illness or business collapse before the penny dropped. Overworking is commonly used as a distraction from the strains and challenges of intimacy. It can seem the ideal solution for someone who struggles with such a close relationship but cannot be alone. Companionship in the office provides a kind of pseudo intimacy, satisfying the hunger for connection and eliminating loneliness, yet maintaining a semblance of control. For neurotic overachievers who fear the strong feelings and messiness of intimacy, work offers alternative relationships. For them, intimacy in and of itself does not seem to achieve anything. In marriage there is a sense of, 'I've won this person, he/she already admires me.' There are no obvious targets to aim for or signs to mark success – no financial triumph or contracts won. And, as with Andrew, overachievers may be frustrated when their spouses refuse to bestow on them the admiration they are used to. Married life fails to satisfy their insatiable need for praise and validation, leaving them to question the point of it.

There are many benefits for overachievers, not only for themselves but also for the companies they work for. The financial rewards can provide a luxurious lifestyle for their family, which is difficult to forsake. Combine this with the emotional needs to manage their internal world, and the prospect of change is daunting. Small changes rather than big ones are more realistic. The first step is recognising that overachieving is causing more problems than it solves.

Here are questions to ask yourself if you think your ambitions risk harming you, your career or people close to you:

- Do you feel guilty if you relax?
- Does any setback leave you believing that all previous successes have been lost?
- Are your excessive work hours having a negative effect on your personal and family life?
- Are you suffering mental or physical symptoms as a result of overwork?
- Do you find it nearly impossible to imagine reducing work to any degree?
- Do you judge colleagues and underlings harshly for not living up to your standards and efforts?
- Do you rely on a 'win' to lift your mood?

If your answers alarm you, try to identify the origins of your motivations. Are they driven by your internal world and personal history or by external factors – competition from colleagues, pressure from management or the culture of your employer?

If you set unreasonably high expectations for yourself, enlist the help of a close colleague or coach to help you gain perspective. Face the consequences of your working habits on your health and personal relationships. How you treat others is often a reflection of your relationship with yourself. When you find yourself irritated by colleagues, recognise that you might be as harsh on them as you are on yourself.

Tolerating the anxieties and uncomfortable feelings that will arise when you inhibit the compulsion to overwork will be crucial. Mind/body techniques such as meditation or yoga can help slow your thinking in order to be less impulsive. Recognise that failure and setbacks are inevitable in life, and that they help you to develop professionally and personally.

### *Externally driven*

Those whose motivations are externally driven are more likely to recognise that they have fallen into an unhealthy predicament. Such people often do well during the first few years in their profession but when the reality dawns of what is required to gain extra levels of promotion they conclude it is not worth the stress. Some, however, can be reluctant to find fault with their organisations and too readily accept the blame. Yet if such extreme expectations are coming from the organisation and not yourself, you may question if the job is really for you. Take time to consider how this work culture impinges on your personal life and well-being. If the cost is too high, consider your position.

As one woman who left investment banking at 30, said to me: 'Having achieved real wealth I realised it hadn't made me happy. As my head hit the pillow a voice said, "You don't have to do this anymore". I felt totally released. On achieving mastery, I realised the thrill is gone.'

What helped her decide was her capacity to reflect, to think matters through.

### Internally driven

Individuals whose motivations are more internal, who are unconsciously trying to solve a deeper psychological conflict, are more likely to push ahead no matter the cost. Simply leaving their job would be of little help since they would likely carry the work pattern to the next. Here, a deeper investigation is required.

Ask yourself, for example, if work distracts you from dealing with difficulties in your personal relationships. Or, better still, ask your spouse or people close to you what they think. It might be that your contact with colleagues provides the limited amount of intimacy you are able to tolerate. If this is the case, do not be harsh on yourself. Instead, find the compassion you need to understand your limits. Having conscious awareness does not always imply that you can overcome psychological barriers but it can help to accept them.

It can be a long and difficult road to rescue oneself from extreme overachieving. First understand its origins, then take small steps. As a start, cut your efforts from 200 per cent to 190 per cent . . .

# 5

# Personality clashes – what part do you play in them?

Before I specialised in business, I saw many married couples for relationship therapy. Usually, each person would arrive for the initial session with the same agenda – eager to get their side of the story across to convince me they had been treated unfairly by the other. Each imagined that it was for me to correct their spouse's wrong thinking and behaviour. Normally I crushed their fantasies of victory immediately.

'I can save you a lot of time and money,' I would say. 'I'm not interested in who is to blame as much as I am curious about how each of you contributes to a marriage, knowingly or not, that makes you both miserable.'

The disappointment on their faces would be writ large. It also tended to leave them both even more determined to set the record straight, each believing they were the exception to my shared-contribution approach and I would change my tune once I heard their tales of woe. More time, more money. We carried on.

An amusing illustration of this occurred in *Ozark*, the Netflix television drama series. Its leading couple, who have fallen into criminality by laundering money for a drug cartel, are shown visiting their therapist, having arrived in separate cars. During the session, the therapist sides with the husband,

Marty, and his wife Wendy is left defeated. After the session they return to their respective cars but Marty waits for Wendy to depart. Once she has driven away he nips back into the therapist's house and slips her extra cash as payment for favouring him. But in a subsequent episode, Wendy, who also has a criminal mind, adopts the same tactic. The only winner here is the equally corrupt therapist.

It has been said that in marriage one has a choice: to either be right or happy. Here is a tip I heard from a vicar when marrying a couple: 'When you win an argument, remember that your prize is to go to bed with the person who has lost the argument. Congratulations!'

When it comes to conflict resolution, business partnerships can learn much from the psychological insights of marital therapy that rescue couples heading full speed for divorce. Facing the disappointment and frustrations of an 'imperfect partnership' or being unable to resolve disputes, are common themes for both. Typically, business partnerships begin because of similarities of interest and ambition between individuals, and often close friendships. Yet their real strength derives from bringing together different skills and personality traits, which, when combined, have the potential to create a successful enterprise. Each partner provides something the other lacks. These differences, however, can also lead to friction. As in a romantic relationship that begins with excitement, a sense of magic and belief that 'we can achieve anything together', a more complex reality eventually kicks in as difficult, crucial decisions need to be made and contentious issues arise. Partners might discover traits in the other they had not bargained for, such as controlling behaviour leading to power struggles, a short temper or lack of application. Instead of finding the other a useful ally, they can end up trashing each other's contribution or feel frustrated that he or she does not appreciate their input. As both retreat further into their respective positions, they become more polarised and begin to act as contenders rather than partners. They have the potential to bring out the best in one another, but also the worst. And there is nothing like working closely to expose our most unpleasant sides. Clients have said to me words to the effect of: 'It's not just my partner that's the problem, it's my behaviour I find appalling.'

Business and marital partnerships end when they have run out of steam and exhausted potential solutions to their problems. No one plans to fail at either kind of alliance – indeed, few take the time to consider what could go wrong. In fairness, of course, spending too much time planning for the worst-case scenario can kill a business almost before it has begun. Optimism is, after all, an essential component of enterprise and vision. Yet the eventual parting can be surprisingly painful. People whose partnerships have disintegrated often describe the ending as a cocktail of loss, anger and sadness – which is sometimes as painful as a divorce.

So how can the lessons of couple therapy be applied to working partnerships? The answer is by also examining them as a circular dynamic with multiple contributing factors rather than a one-way or linear explanation of a single cause leading to a disastrous outcome. Clients, as with married couples, have arrived at my consulting room convinced culpability resides entirely with the other partner. My approach aims to encourage them to expand their perspective, be surprised by what they discover and curious to learn more. I often comment: 'There is no point coming to see me just to tell what you already know.'

The first step is to establish a shared reality where both parties can agree on what has happened, however minimal their agreement might be. Then I hear each one's perspective. Next we begin investigating how each individual, unknowingly, brings out the unwanted traits in the other. The emphasis is on encouraging each to be curious about the other's motivations and take responsibility for their contribution. I also explain that the advantage of recognising your part in the conflict is that you then have more control. It is easier to alter your own behaviour than your partner's.

Enough of the theory, let's see the method in action. A common tension in partnerships is when one individual is more concerned with detail and operational aspects while the other is more creative or better at promoting the business. This was the case for two founders of a media start-up who sought my help. One was meticulous, obsessional and focused on detail and organisation. He had become frustrated by his partner who was more laissez-faire but creative and effective at selling their product. The business required both their talents but they had ceased appreciating the other's contribution and instead begun treating one another as a threat. The obsessive partner felt the creative was unreliable, while the latter felt he was constantly being 'nagged.'

After seeking to create a safe atmosphere in which to explore the contentious issues, I heard each side separately before bringing them together to explain how each contributed to a circular dynamic resulting in spiralling tensions. These sessions involved probing more deeply into their early lives to understand the origins of their anxieties and motivations. This part of the process can be done either in individual sessions or, if the parties prefer, in joint sessions where they can learn more about the other's background and psychological influences. Creating such a shared reality helps individuals see the conflict in a context where both play a part and removes the sting of blame, the need to personalise and desire to attack back. Once individuals are assured they are safe from unfair accusations, they are more likely to explore and find alternative ways of operating and solutions that work for both.

As we continued to talk, it became clear that the media duo were pushing each other further into a damaging pattern. When the creative one ignored details and deadlines, his partner became more anxious and obsessional to alleviate his anxiety. Simultaneously, the creative felt criticised by his partner's insistence on time-keeping and, in response, became more withdrawn and aggressive. This increased distance in turn left the operational partner insecure and eventually even more obsessional – and so the vicious cycle intensified. Each dealt with their anxiety differently: one by being obsessional, the other by becoming distant and avoiding details that felt uncomfortable. In other words, in lessening their own anxiety, they were making the other feel worse. Rather than being able to appreciate their differences and various contributions, they infuriated one another.

I discovered that the creative had repeatedly distanced

himself from other close relationships, beginning with his mother whom he experienced as suffocating, and continuing in his marriage because intimacy made him panic. The obsessive, on the other hand, feared failure. His father had lost the family's fortune as a result of poor business decisions and he was determined not to repeat that. All this was brought to the table for examination. Enlarging the context in this way provided explanations, deepened understanding and reduced resentment and accusations. To arrive at a positive and lasting impact, both had to understand the other's motivations, tolerate their own anxieties and change their behaviour.

Following the individual and joint sessions, they could acknowledge their lifelong friendship and remember what brought them together initially. It was their friendship as much as the business's future that had first motivated them to confront uncomfortable truths about themselves and see me. Such motivation to solve the problem, incidentally, is crucial to the success of this approach. The two could also again appreciate, rather than be irritated by, the other's input and thereby develop a closer working relationship. Once this was established, the obsessive was less anxious and more relaxed, and the creative felt less under attack and more willing to listen and collaborate. By recognising how each contributed to the problem, they could take responsibility for turning the cycle from a destructive to a constructive one.

When we refer to people we work with as 'colleagues' we disguise the fact that we are actually dealing with relationships – ones that sometimes wind us up or touch a nerve, not unlike other close relationships in our lives. Initially, we treat such work relationships as transactional or functional ones, where we anticipate a clear agreement on what is expected. Over time the relationship develops to one which is symbiotic, or mutually dependent. Here, trust, collaboration and dealing with disagreements become crucial if we are to be successful.

Workplace conflicts, from quickly forgotten spats to bitter disputes or long, simmering feuds, are as inevitable as they are in any sphere of human activity. One difference, however, compared with clashes with a spouse or close family member, is that the colleagues at loggerheads are not intimate. A spat at home is usually short-lived because you know that beneath the current anger there is mutual love and respect. Such personal relationships are more meaningful and therefore the motivation to find a solution is greater. In addition, the security of family life allows for more charged conversations, whereas at work the price of losing control of one's emotions can be high. However, when resentments and other strong feelings are not expressed directly they find an indirect outlet, for example, through passive-aggressive behaviour, often with damaging consequences, or they are pushed internally resulting in anxiety or depression.

At work, we are also more likely to be stung by an off-the-cuff remark from someone whom we do not necessarily realise is outspoken or tactless. Someone might not think their tone of voice sounds more aggressive than intended, while at the same time someone else is left feeling that they have been attacked or accused unfairly. As a consequence, we are less likely to give the other person the benefit of the doubt and more likely to misinterpret their words or motives, believing they may be after our jobs, perhaps or pursuing their own interest. Furthermore, once we have judged a colleague harshly, we tend to put him or her in a derogatory pigeon hole and rarely have the time or inclination to reconsider our opinion. By being quick to find fault in others, or judging them harshly, we attempt to rid ourselves of guilt, shame or feelings of inadequacy.

In turn, it requires tremendous effort to make others change their view of us. If as a boss you are rightly accused of overt favouritism, for example, you would then need to demonstrate a commitment to equality and fairness in clear ways and over time to convince staff you have changed. Too often, people believe that if they have altered their thinking, others will miraculously know. Put aside any resentment and frustration towards colleagues for not appreciating how hard you might have worked to address this – the onus is on you to convince others you have modified your approach.

When individual disputes flare up our default tendency is to assume the other party is at fault or even that they are 'bad or mad', simply because they disagree and irritate us. Although this attitude may soothe our fragile egos, behind this deluded thinking is a belief that there is nothing for us to learn or correct and we miss an opportunity to recognise our blind spots. So, before leaping to conclusions that may only exacerbate matters, first consider your own part in the circumstances and the larger context. Are they saying something that you do not want to hear? Are they saying something that needs to be addressed? Do you fear they may expose you in a bad light?

Take the time to discover where the other person is coming from, discern their motives, be curious about their ideas and have the maturity to consider opposing views without feeling threatened.

Ask yourself further questions. Why is this person getting under my skin? Is this interaction familiar? Is the tension arising from my internal world – i.e. prompted by past experiences? Alternatively, am I ignoring a potentially destructive situation because I fear conflict or the consequences of speaking out? Or am I simply overwhelmed and lacking the energy to face the issue?

Clashes in the office can echo conflicts from our childhood. This explains why for some people minor disputes can feel bigger or more significant than they actually are. Being ignored by the boss can be disappointing, for example, but when confused with neglect one has suffered in childhood, it can feel devastating. Individuals who are highly anxious or who had to remain hyper-vigilant in their early lives to prepare themselves for potential harm can be unable to distinguish between benign disagreements and more serious ones. They are not just quick to spot and react to tensions but anticipating a clash can mean they misread situations and see conflict where none exists.

Our families are responsible for setting a blueprint in our minds for how we perceive and navigate conflicts, which we then bring to work. Take the time to think about how conflicts were dealt with in your family. Were arguments heated and loud? Did disagreements feel contained or out of control? Were individuals shown respect, or ignored or excluded as a result? Did arguments lead to resolutions or did they make matters worse? Were difficult issues talked about or swept under the carpet? Were feelings expressed directly or indirectly through passive-aggressive behaviour? Did you feel safe when the emotional temperature ran high?

If conflicts led to dangerous or even violent outcomes in your family, any differing of views subsequently might feel threatening. If this describes your family history, think back to how you responded. Did you meet fire with fire, run for cover or attempt to protect the person who was being attacked?

Now consider how these experiences influence your response to disputes at work. Do you find yourself playing the same part in your professional life that you had in your family? Perhaps you were the rescuer, the scapegoat or mediator. Do you adopt the same role at work? If the answer is a resounding 'yes,' then ask yourself if it is working well for you or not.

Here, for instance, is the blueprint that I inherited. My parents were Hungarian immigrants in California. They argued often when I was growing up but only in Hungarian, so the meaning of their rows was a mystery to me. It is often the case in immigrant families that it is the eldest who speaks the parents' language in order to translate, while the youngest – in this case me – is left out of the loop. So although I hadn't a clue what they were arguing about, I saw that tempers ran high, as did the volume of their voices. Nothing appeared to improve after an argument – quite the contrary: as I observed their bad moods everyone seemed worse off and retreated to separate rooms.

As I was a helpful child, my first approach was to try to

understand what was going on. Gathering all my strength, I would stand up, look them both in the eye and demand they speak English. At this point, they would pause, momentarily look towards me in disbelief and then immediately revert to shouting in Hungarian. I eventually gave up.

As a result, I came to believe that disagreements quickly escalate and leave everyone worse off, including and especially myself. I was also baffled as to how to resolve them. This undoubtedly influenced my eventual desire to pursue a freelance, self-employed career where I was less likely to be faced with interpersonal conflict. Learning to be objective and reflective, and even welcoming differences of opinion, came only after years of self-analysis and determination.

We not only bring these psychological blueprints into our professional lives but also our strategies for resolving conflicts. While these may have helped us (or not, as in my case) when we were young, the same strategies can have the effect of escalating rather than reducing tensions in the workplace, as this next case illustrates.

Joan, a warm and engaging single woman in her early thirties who worked for a wealth management company, employed a strategy she learnt as a child to prevent conflicts. To her dismay, however, it had the opposite effect.

She came to me at her wits' end after reading an article I had written for the *Financial Times* on conflict in the workplace. There was no doubt in her mind that she needed professional help to deal with what she perceived were unfair accusations. Her softly spoken manner and willingness to examine her part did not align with allegations of bullying behaviour that had been made against her. I was curious to hear more.

Talented and intelligent as she was, she could not understand why her attempts to be extremely accommodating and supportive of her team had backfired so badly, leaving her feeling misunderstood and unfairly attacked. Her approach was to give her team plenty of flexibility and responsibility, while at the same time communicating with them regularly. In return, she assumed they would meet their performance targets. An unpleasant incident, however, crystallised the limitations of her strategy and prompted her to begin questioning herself. One day her staff left work early for the pub even though an important project had not been completed. She thought she had been more than generous in giving her staff latitude, yet clearly she was being taken for a ride and was furious.

'When I pushed them on this I faced a backlash in terms of, "You're being too harsh," "Your standards are too high,"' she told me with frustration in her voice. 'I felt like I was dealing with kids. They were being unfair, and that was what hurt me.'

One of her team even defied her instructions to complete a project on time. 'In my sector that is unheard of; if you're supposed to do something, you do it. He was saying how unreasonable I was, how I was too direct and not saying things nicely. That escalated to the point where he said, "You have a history in this firm of not treating your juniors well, I can complain about you [to management] and you won't be able to do anything about it."'

When management appeared to validate the employee's view, Joan felt utterly defeated. She was astounded that the employee would threaten her after she gave him so much freedom and that management did not support her. Clearly, her attempts to please everyone in the hope of avoiding conflict and achieving results had failed. Although everyone had a part to play in rising hostilities, Joan had an instinct that she had unknowingly stirred the pot. Fearful of repeating the same scenario, she came to me determined to make sense of it all.

We soon discovered that a similar dynamic – where she had been accommodating yet treated unfairly – had operated in her family. She had often been compared by her parents with her sister, who was lauded for her academic achievements. These would be used in an attempt to motivate Joan to achieve more but had unintended consequences, in that she believed her parents sided with her sister even when she, Joan, was in the right.

She leant forward in her chair, enthused by the connection she had made, as she told me: 'The frustration I felt at my job was not dissimilar from the frustration I felt as a kid. It was, "Hold on, hear me out, this is what happened, you're treating me unfairly." It's quite similar to what happened at work. I was trying to explain my position and no one wanted to listen. They automatically assumed my sister or the team or whoever is complaining about me, is right. So there are definitely parallels – noticing that in itself is powerful.'

Her parents both worked full time and, as a child, Joan had concluded that the last thing they would want to deal with after a long working day was squabbling between their daughters.

So, in order to please them, she became the one to solve rather than create problems. 'If you're the kid who accommodates so that the problem goes away, you make them happy,' she explained. 'I do that at work as well.'

Recognising the parallels meant she could inhibit old habits, ask herself pertinent questions and change her approach to managing her team.

'I was too accommodating,' she said, realising that this had created rather than prevented conflict. 'Maybe that's why deadlines started slipping and people's performance started getting sloppier. They noticed I didn't mean what I said until I started really meaning it, by which time they were saying: "Hold on, what's wrong? For three months I've been delaying the work and you've been fine, so what's wrong right now?"'

During a period of intense coaching sessions, we examined alternative ways of managing her team. We agreed that her approach should provide more structure and that she should work more closely with her staff. Later she told me how things had gone.

'We agree a deadline and if it's not met we have a chat and make sure it doesn't slip again. I'm happier now and more trusting of people. Relationships are the way they should be – less emotional and more professional.'

Like Joan, the strains and pressures of organisational life can reduce us to feeling like a child. For those who have been traumatised – and that does include most of us, to a greater or lesser extent, as I will explain – clashes can rekindle old traumas. Ordinary work disappointments, such as losing out on a promotion, being treated unfairly or being excluded from a work group can reopen early wounds, leaving someone overwhelmed with incomprehensible feelings. Self-loathing and feelings of unworthiness can overtake us. For some, this can even extend to shame, a sense of not deserving to exist.

As I described previously, trauma describes a much broader range of emotional and physical responses to painful experiences than is usually acknowledged. Most commonly, it is a reaction to insecure attachments to our parents or caregivers in the first few years of life. If these people were either chaotic, negligent, ambivalent or anxious when responding to our early needs, it can have lasting effects on how we respond to emotions and relationships – indeed, all aspects of our lives. The mind rushes to protect us from unbearable feelings of grief, hopelessness, pain or rage by numbing or disassociating from emotions and developing strategies to distance us from these unwanted memories.

These traumas do not disappear but rather remain in our bodies, albeit unconsciously, and can be reignited at moments of tension at work. This explains how relatively minor disagreements or a hurtful remark can send you reeling when they inflame early experiences of humiliation, helplessness or abandonment. Indeed, the workplace for many can become an excruciating experience.

Charlotte is an attractive young woman with an outgoing and appealing personality who had established a web design business with a partner, Louise. The story she related to me illustrates how early trauma can easily be reignited in a working partnership.

Charlotte grew up as an only child and her father was either absent or a destructive presence. He had a general attitude that 'nothing is ever good enough,' she told me. As a result, she felt rejected if she underperformed academically or indeed in any area of her life. Her mother was subservient, always giving in to her domineering husband, but despite this acquiescence, Charlotte remembers the atmosphere around the family as one of tension and unhappiness.

Those memories, firmly absorbed into her psyche, came back to haunt her in the partnership with Louise. In particular, she felt re-traumatised when her partner's casual remarks felt accusatory, echoing her father.

'When it [a project] was something simple, she'd say: "God, has it taken you all day to write that thing?" That statement would make me feel incredibly flustered and that self-doubt could stay with me for days.'

Charlotte explained how tensions escalated when each attempted to assume the top position while the other was absent on maternity leave. Vying for power had led to clashes between them as first Charlotte and then Louise, had returned to work after their leave. Rather than having the empathy to appreciate the difficulty of re-establishing one's professional role after such a break, each used the opportunity to gain dominance over the other.

Charlotte said: 'My most disempowered moments were when I was coming back from maternity leave and unsure of my identity. I lost my role in the company and that made me feel incredibly sensitive and she took advantage of that period and wasn't sympathetic.'

Yet Charlotte took the opportunity to reverse matters when it came her partner's turn for maternity leave, using the time to cement her position in the business. With her partner absent, Charlotte could be the 'face of the business.' Her confidence grew and her performance improved. She admitted that she ensured Louise knew her place on her return – and this wasn't as an equal partner. Whereas Charlotte was cut to the quick by criticism, Louise's vulnerability centred on feeling left out. By not including her in discussions and forming alliances with other people in the company, Charlotte, albeit subconsciously, ensured that she maintained power over Louise.

Reflecting on her behaviour during Louise's absence, she said: 'I was clawing my way back having felt disempowered after two years of feeling rubbish. I now realise she was in a fragile place and probably also feeling all those things.'

There were pros and cons to their dynamic. While in one regard their competitive relationship improved the business, each keeping the other on her toes if one perceived the other was underperforming, such criticism also took its toll. And in Charlotte's mind, there could be only one head of the business. This mindset originated in her family, which impressed on her that if she was not the powerful one she would be the victim.

'I now recognise my oversensitivity comes from having a bullying, critical father and no strong female role model,' she reflected. 'The feeling of failure is so horrific and so abhorrent. It's easy for self-doubt to creep in and then I feel completely unsafe, ungrounded, worthless, totally destabilised. I didn't see much of my mum standing up for herself at all. So that kind of bullying was just absorbed.'

Louise, who would lash out when she felt insecure, touched that deep nerve over criticism in Charlotte. Yet when Charlotte withdrew to protect herself, Louise in turn felt left out and angry. This was how they unknowingly hurt each other and the business.

Matters improved during the coronavirus lockdown of 2020 as they both worked from home and had reduced contact. Even before this period, they had been heading in separate work trajectories. Although this distancing reduced the tensions, they risked losing the collaboration needed for the business to develop and prosper. Their tensions might not have been entirely resolved but, with the insight gained, Charlotte was able to view matters more objectively, increase her sensitivity towards Louise and improve their relationship.

Those who have been traumatised develop survival strategies to cope with the resulting strong feelings, as we have seen in many of the case studies in this book. Presenting an image of self-sufficiency or controlling your immediate environment so as not to have to deal with sudden surprises are common ones. Workaholism and perfectionism also, or ensuring others are dependent on you to ensure you are not dependent on anybody. Think about strategies you have learnt to distance yourself from harmful or hurtful situations in your family. Perhaps you said little or behaved impeccably so as not to aggravate tensions or potentially volatile situations. Did you learn that tuning into people's needs to the neglect of your own ensured you would have functioning and more attentive caregivers?

Dr Franz Ruppert, Professor of Psychology at the University of Applied Sciences in Munich, has written extensively about trauma. He theorises that while a part of us remains traumatised, another part develops strategies to keep the unwanted emotions concealed. Alongside these there is a third 'healthy side,' which remains unharmed by the trauma. This part enables us to tolerate our feelings, gain clarity, face painful truths and difficult situations. When in touch with our healthier side we are more compassionate with ourselves and able to experience positive emotions, such as joy and passion and have a sense of agency in our lives. Our best response when feeling traumatised at work is to tune into this healthy and mature side.

**Change Your Narrative:** Dealing with clashes in the workplace requires you to change your narrative, for the story you tell yourself largely determines whether the conflict is resolved, continues or escalates. This story is more than an explanation – it provokes feelings that can either make you feel safe or threatened. And if your explanation is fixed, so will be your potential solutions. Be open to alternative narratives. Gain perspective and separate the past trauma from the present dispute. Respond to the latter, not the former.

**Be curious:** To do this you will need to be curious about the other person's motivations as well as your own and from this a new perspective, or version of events, can emerge together with alternative solutions. Instead of leaping to sinister explanations, try giving them the benefit of the doubt. He/she may have no interest in sabotaging your work or taking your job, for instance. When we feel threatened, we are more likely to make gross generalisations about the other person and dismiss their good work and positive traits. Put yourself in their shoes and try to understand the issue from their perspective. Create enough of a shared reality and safety between you to allow for these different and more constructive conversations.

**Be honest:** And don't forget to identify how your behaviour might trigger the other person to react in ways that increase tension. This might not be easy to spot if your motivations are unconscious. One question I like to ask people, which often makes them squirm in their seat, is: 'Why would you repeat a behaviour that you know irritates your colleague and raises tension?' Often the answers lie in our subconscious but we refuse to pay attention.

Although consciously disliking the conflict, your unconscious might be acting out historic hostilities. Such 'familiarity' can be as comforting as a warm duvet but do not succumb. To gain insight, you will need to stop blaming the other and resist the urge to justify your behaviour. It may feed your ego but it will not get you far.

I recall a client who told me how, as part of a long-running tension with his partner, he had withheld giving praise to him, knowing this was precisely what he craved. Yet eventually he turned the narrative around, from 'my partner is treating me unfairly' to 'I'm touching a nerve in him that hurts.' He then began to acknowledge his partner's good work. This shift in thinking and behaviour was enough to put their relationship, and the business, on a sounder course.

**Be objective:** Try not to personalise it if others are critical of your work. They are probably genuinely responding to your performance, your work habits or commenting on a specific piece of work – it is not about *you* as a person. Weigh the criticism as objectively as you can and if you think there is substance to it, try to improve. Of course there are times when the other person is primarily in the wrong but acknowledging your part, even if it's only 10 per cent of the problem, can be the start of resolving most conflicts.

Once you change your behaviour, whether as a result of criticism or to try to resolve a dispute, observe the results. If the change is positive, it will enhance your confidence and likely improve your relationship with the other person. Do not underestimate how much people will appreciate your altered stance. Not only will it build empathy but also demonstrate courage and strength of character on your part. There will always be difficult personalities and contentious issues at work, so the earlier you learn how to deal with them, the better your career prospects.

# 6

# Paranoia, envy and the seeds of irrational conflict

'You hire clever people but you don't want them to be too clever in case they outshine you. The truth is, I liked it when they were doing well – but not too well.'

*A leading UK chief executive*

Much has been written about conflict in the workplace but unfortunately, too much of it assumes that individuals are unfailingly rational beings willing to face difficult issues and find a compromise. While certain approaches work for more psychologically mature individuals, something different is often needed to tackle the many irrational, extreme or long-standing disputes in the workplace.

Abnormal behaviour such as repeated lying, sabotaging others' work, withholding information or spreading malicious gossip is characteristic of people who either cannot control their emotions or are acting out unresolved unconscious conflicts. When such behaviour appears inexplicable, it is often down to hidden motivations, the origin of the dispute having been lost. Paranoia, rage and envy are often the culprits that drive such irrational conduct. Although these are universal emotions, and are not necessarily harmful, the danger is that extreme manifestations of them can make conflict inevitable and lead to immeasurable damage at work.

This chapter will attempt to make sense of more extreme irrational antagonisms, help to distinguish between rational and irrational ones and offer suggestions for dealing with them. A warning first: it must be remembered that the line between rational and irrational is by no means obvious and more a matter of degree than absolute certainty! And while managers do not have to be psychotherapists or psychiatrists, they need to be able to identify which conflicts can be resolved and those where damage limitation is the only useful response.

While being suspicious of or hostile towards those we believe have undermined us is not necessarily harmful, difficulties arise when such feelings are expressed indirectly and vindictively. Such is the case with passive-aggressive behaviour, where undigested thoughts and feelings result in destructive behaviour. When the underlying motivation is unconscious, provoked by historic and/or unresolved traumas or conflicts, individuals can be unaware of what they are doing or why. Rage, for example, may be constrained and stored, only to erupt elsewhere where inevitably it becomes more difficult to identify its origins and manage.

The pressure to excel, alongside the insecurities and strong feelings that office life provokes, creates a breeding ground for irrational thoughts and reactions. The workplace is a theatre where everyone is acting out their own unique family drama while simultaneously attempting to co-operate and deliver results. While there appears to be one external reality, there are multiple internal ones to contend with.

At moments of tension and stress our thinking narrows – we become defensive and locate the fault in the other rather than ourselves. When we conclude we are being attacked, we feel justified in defending ourselves and hitting back rather than trying to make sense of the situation. But it is precisely sense-making that is required, not only to resolve disputes but also to turn potentially destructive clashes into constructive ones.

Individuals must confront their internal world if they become embroiled in a dispute, and try to make sense of irrational behaviour on their part and that of their adversary. Those who have the maturity to regulate their emotions are better equipped to recognise their irrational thoughts and inhibit the impulse to act on them. Their distorted thinking can be thought about and processed, a capacity that will enhance their performance and further their career. We also have to decide whether it is worth pursuing a resolution at all – but more of that later.

So let's begin by exploring envy – a common example of irrational thinking that plays a much bigger role in conflict at work than is acknowledged.

Envy is one of the most shameful feelings to admit and, because of the secrecy involved, challenging to manage. While envy damages relationships and operational aspects of organisations, the originator of it is also a casualty. For example, the thrill of witnessing an envied colleague's failure is often followed by guilt for having such ungenerous thoughts. Just read this successful film producer's thoughtful account to me of how envy towards others' success affected him, beginning with a scene we are all familiar with – the Academy Awards ceremony in Hollywood.

'The Oscars is a good example [of envy] when the camera is on the person who hasn't won. There are always those being happy for others' success and, of course, lying to their core. There *are* people who thrive on other people's success but they are pretty few.' He continued: 'It is a horrible feeling when you see someone release a film and you are willing it to do badly. It can make you feel very disgusted with yourself. You feel deep down that it is wrong and it doesn't really enhance your success [either]. But it is quite prevalent and the schadenfreude when someone gets a stinker of a review – I guess it protects you because you're not the only one getting stinking reviews.

'Initially it can give you an adrenaline rush but then it induces a sense of self-loathing. What starts out as aggressive feelings outwards, turns inward on yourself. You are feeling rotten because of what you have become, so that even when you are successful you can undermine that sense of pleasure because somehow [envy] spoils the process.'

Our earliest experiences of envy originate with feelings of insecurity and perceived scarcity in early childhood, leading to sibling rivalry, which is then replaced by envy in adulthood and taken into the workplace. Insecurity, alongside competition with colleagues, can reignite these childhood emotions, fuelling them until they become out of control. Sibling rivalry can be resolved as we grow and mature or alternatively it can escalate to feelings of hatred and rage. *Succession*, the HBO television series, provides a compelling and rich picture of the latter. The sons and daughter of a father who is the ruthless, narcissistic and tyrannical head of a media empire compete not just for power in the organisation and ultimately the top spot, but more deeply for recognition and affection from the old man. They continually plot and manoeuvre to gain advantage and their father's approval, while also seeking to denigrate a sibling and destroy his or her prospects. They are compelled as much by their rage towards one another as desire for power.

Envy is not uniformly destructive – in its more benign form, conscious envy can motivate individuals to better themselves to achieve what they admire in others. Indeed, it is often what pushes students to excel in business schools, for example, or helps drive individuals to leadership positions. However, while it is possible for conscious envy to be contained and turned into healthy competition, envy is most dangerous and destructive when pushed into the unconscious where it cannot be examined. Here it transforms into rage and hatred towards the person who has achieved what the envious person desires and is acted out in spiteful or sarcastic attacks. Jenny Eclair, the writer and comedian, described in an interview with the *Guardian* newspaper in 2020 how it felt as if there could be only one winner among the women performers on the UK comedy circuit in the 1980s when there were only a handful competing for the top gigs.

She said: 'We were all scrabbling for this tiny window of opportunity, and as soon as somebody got through, it was firmly shut again. I really liked all the other women on the circuit, until they got more famous than me, then I hated them. That's the truth of it.'

Destructive envy is more than merely desiring what

someone else has accomplished or gained, it is also wanting to destroy what they have achieved because their success has come to feel like your misfortune. Rather than learning from the person's success or recognising their hard work, you belittle their achievement and/or believe you have been unfairly treated. And this, you conclude, justifies retaliation. Spreading malicious gossip about a person, criticising or ignoring their ideas, or withholding information from them can seem safe undermining strategies because they are easily hidden from others. It is precisely this secrecy, however, that makes it difficult to identify and thus more insidious.

From an organisational point of view, one of the most debilitating aspects of envy is that it obstructs learning and collaboration. Tanya Menon, Professor of Management and Human Resources at Fisher College of Business, Ohio State University, has studied envy in the workplace. Her research reveals that people prefer to learn new techniques, ideas or strategies from people outside their own companies – even from rival ones – rather than from within their own organisation. Her explanation of why such 'outside' learning is more effective comes down to envy.

'From my work, I noticed that people tend to learn much more readily from external competitors than internal competitors,' she said. 'Most research says that people favour their in-group members, people who share a common identity. But in business we see exactly the opposite. Someone in your own organisation is much more threatening because they directly compete with you for bonuses and promotions. Someone outside the firm doesn't directly compete for the rewards.'

The price of this envy is, of course, high for the organisations and businesses concerned. Instead of training and enlightening their staff themselves with their own personnel, expensive consultants and external trainers have to be brought in. Professor Menon studied the case of one company that had acquired another for its intellectual knowledge and quality of staff, but the takeover had backfired. She explained that when the companies were competitors there was significant learning from each other, but after the combining of the two that mutual interest ceased.

'After the acquisition happened, the outsider became the insider and they started denigrating the very things that they had been admiring initially. This is the interesting thing about envy – it's precisely because something or someone reveals excellence that people do not want to learn from it.'

Envy is not just pervasive in the sense that it occurs at all levels of work and is directed by individuals at colleagues of similar status as well as those above them. Susan Reh, Christian Tröster and Niels Van Quaquebeke of Kühne Logistics University, Hamburg, demonstrated that it is also manifested by individuals in regard to people who are beneath them in an organisation but rising rapidly. They established, through controlled behavioural experiments, that people with a rapidly rising career trajectory attracted envy from people above them whose career path had been slower. One of their conclusions, presented in the *Journal of Applied Psychology* in 2018, was that the senior employees saw their ambitious juniors as a future threat to their status. Furthermore, they would even engage in behaviour to undermine these perceived rivals, particularly when the culture of the company concerned was competitive.

Professor Van Quaquebeke explained to me how, once again, organisations lose out because of envy: 'If you're really good at what you're doing as a boss, you have a steep trajectory [of past progress] and are confident of your abilities, you will have no issue with hiring really good people. But if you're a boss who's had a mixed trajectory, you are more careful when hiring because you definitely don't want anybody to overtake you who may make your precarious position even worse.

'If you hire B-class people there may be a chance that B people will turn out to be A people, so instead you stay on the safe side and think, "I'd rather take C people because I can be sure they're not going to overtake me".'

So even attainment of the ultimate leadership role does not necessarily subdue envy. Successful leadership requires handing over plaudits and reward to underlings, but envy can obstruct a boss's willingness to accept that some staff might be more successful than him or her.

Mark Stein, professor of leadership and management at the University of Leicester in the UK, says business leaders' fear of being usurped by subordinates with outstanding skills and leadership ability also makes envy 'the real issue in leadership succession.'

'If you know you are going to retire, it's difficult to find space in your heart to help someone take on your position and do it well,' he says. 'The real fear is that they can do it better.'

And he adds that for bosses to acknowledge their envy would imply recognising the limits of their own achievements.

A good leader needs to learn to gain satisfaction from the achievements of their staff, rather than seeking it only from personal accomplishments. Knowing that you have supported and played a part in others' success by encouragement or providing opportunities should give a sense of personal achievement. The key is how strongly you identify with your staff and their work – the stronger the identification, the more likely you are to feel a sense of personal satisfaction. This is a challenging transition for many leaders to make, yet necessary in both maximising people's talents and securing their support.

How do we tackle our own envy? If you have the capability to recognise your rage and grievance as envy rather than unfairness, you are better equipped to inhibit the impulse to attack or spread gossip about your object of envy. Thinking about the discomfort rather than acting on it will help you to focus instead on your own ambitions and desires. Begin by trying to understand the origins of your envy. Can you recall a time in your childhood when you envied one of your siblings? How did that affect your relationship? Were you ever envied by a childhood friend or sibling? What did that feel like?

As regards to the envy you currently experience, ask yourself what does the person have that you crave? Is it status or power? Do you envy their talents and skills? Observe how they have achieved their success. Perhaps they know how to position or promote themselves better than you do. Often we fail to appreciate the hard work and sacrifices someone else has made to attain their position.

Envy may be difficult to identify in yourself. If your feelings become so strong as to flip into hatred or rage, or you begin to fantasise about the other person's demise, it is likely you are struggling with it.

Becoming clear about what you envy in a person clarifies what you must work on to achieve it for yourself. The most positive response is to learn from him or her rather than allowing your feeling of entitlement to prevail. Remember that when you choose to undermine someone rather than learn from them, there is no personal growth to be gained – everybody loses. Spare yourself the guilt and self-loathing that usually accompanies envy and instead use it to fire your ambition and direction.

As with envy, paranoia also runs along a wide continuum of being healthy and adaptive at one end to increasingly irrational and finally pathological at the opposite extreme. Healthy paranoia, or what can otherwise be understood as suspicion, is normally based on realistic observations and experiences, though it may also be an adaptive response to past traumatic experiences. Pathological paranoia, however, is removed from reality and can lead to dangerous misunderstandings and organisational damage.

Let's start at the positive end. A reasonable dose of paranoia can be an asset at work. For self-protection it is wise to have a degree of suspicion – even people you trust in one context, for example, might be untrustworthy in the next. Often in business, there is an assumption that you should trust colleagues that you do not know well. Where there is no evidence for trusting a person, it is best to settle for merely building rapport or respect.

Organisations and businesses can also benefit from those with more than a healthy share of paranoia, as Andrew Grove, the late former chief executive of Intel, illustrated in his book *Only the Paranoid Survive*. Their antennae are continually alert to potential threats to a company that others miss, whether it be from competitors, regulators, technology changes, disruptors or shifting consumer trends. In addition, such individuals may have the courage others lack to report suspicious or illegal practices in the workplace.

Further benefits for individuals are posited by Professor Van Quaquebeke, who has also studied paranoia closely. He believes that a functional level of the trait can help people advance to leadership positions. Constantly on alert for potential threats and pitfalls, the paranoid have a heightened sensitivity in social situations and interactions. Consequently, they are better equipped at adapting to the complex arenas of social relations that make up work environments and manoeuvring through them. They quickly absorb management norms and values, are always scanning the environment for threats so as to evade or counter them and adapt their behaviour towards others to avoid being attacked. Furthermore, they demarcate the world into loyal colleagues or enemies and in this way form coalitions, albeit fragile ones. They also, for instance, will support projects as a pre-emptive strategy to ensure others do not turn against them. Professor Van Quaquebeke cites, as an example from his own world, an academic who has included colleagues in the bibliography of a study they had not contributed to in order to ensure they would not criticise his work. Combining all these characteristics with the heightened sensibility to risks facing a company referred to by Andrew Grove makes these people formidable candidates for leadership positions.

The following case illustrates how persistent hyper-vigilance, or a mild case of paranoia, can be a response to earlier traumatic experiences. It also demonstrates how it can be both a help and a hindrance to one's career and professional development.

Robert is a 38-year-old highly successful investment banker, introverted in nature but nevertheless well liked and respected by colleagues. When we met at his office in London, I found him to be quietly spoken but with manners and a charm that quickly endeared him to me. Although a financier by profession, his mind operated more like a philosopher – a deep thinker wishing to understand more about life.

His reluctance to be 'in the spotlight,' however, had stymied his potential. He was judgemental of others who had been promoted but held himself back in this regard because he believed he would be seen as a 'selfish climber' by colleagues. Projecting his own thoughts into others, he thought they would be as harsh on him as he was on them.

Robert's cautious nature and constant hyper-vigilance had helped him become a successful analyst and good team player but matters came to a head when the bank encouraged him to pursue a leadership role, as he explained. 'Being super careful as to what you say [to other people] is helpful. For me, it's like driving a car with the hand brake on – it's probably safer but you're going very slowly. You reach a point where you should be able to drop your guard a little bit when you achieve job security, but then this [hyper-vigilance] becomes a hindrance.

'Sometimes you're afraid of being afraid. If I don't appear

super confident, how's that going to look? Will clients wonder if this guy knows what he's doing? This becomes a vicious cycle, I'm more afraid of appearing afraid than the actual substance of it, which is low risk.'

His fear of taking a leadership position and worry over being seen as weak or fearful stemmed from his relationship with his domineering father, who was judgemental towards successful people that he perceived as being 'climbers' and whom he dismissed as unethical. Furthermore, he exhibited a passive-aggressive anger that in childhood left Robert fearful of his father's displeasure. Yet because he was uncertain as to what triggered this anger, the son's only option was to remain hyper-vigilant.

'He never screamed at me, he was more a psychological bully, passive-aggressive. You could do something and never know what it was, and then he could be very angry. He was very much a "man" – if you're a real man you're never weak or insecure.

'You always had to give him space – I couldn't challenge him because that would be dangerous. I had to act as if he was the most important person because my father had to be the man. I never feel fully like an adult. I'm 38, but sometimes I feel like a kid.'

His father's character created internal conflicts for Robert as an adult. He was eager to progress in his career but simultaneously feared his father's harsh judgement of successful people and this outweighed his ambition to climb the hierarchy at work. Yet he was also torn by thoughts of being seen as weak or fearful – traits that would equally anger his father.

As a result, at work he recreated the same hierarchy as existed in his family, allowing others to lead so as to avoid potential retaliation from them should he usurp their position. Unconsciously, he transferred his dread of his father's anger to authority figures in the bank. His promotional prospects were stunted because he anticipated being the target of others' condemnation, imagining they would judge him a 'climber' lacking morality and ethical leadership. His paranoid thoughts not only obstructed his advancement but also his relationships at work – he remained guarded, not allowing colleagues to get close, which left him isolated and lonely at times. He acknowledged that his excessive worry and misguided thinking took up an inordinate amount of energy that he could not maintain in the long run.

'I'm highly ambitious and trying to do well, but I'm doing it in a way that never compromises with this moral purity, which is impossible. That conflict is the story of my life – you want to get ahead but while at the same time complying with these highly unrealistic expectations.'

By examining his issues with me, Robert came to recognise that he was reacting to internal conflicts rather than external ones. He located the source of his anxieties with his father and began to cease replicating his family relationships in the workplace. Separating the past from the present helped him to become more relaxed, confident and take more risks. It also freed the mental space for him to consider how he would like his working life to develop in the future.

As this case exemplifies, while a degree of vigilance is healthy for any individual or organisation, if taken to an extreme it can slip into irrational thinking when our imagination, as opposed to reality, dictates what we think and how we respond. We are all at risk of being more driven by our interpretation of events than what is really happening, but people with a strong tendency towards paranoia see disapproval, potential threats and betrayal everywhere. Their fear means they often misread situations and others' intensions – and clashes result.

The more seriously paranoid believe they are being harmed or exploited at work and so hit back and blame others, thereby igniting tensions. And when colleagues react with anger in turn, it only confirms their fantasies of being treated unfairly. To exacerbate matters, they do not easily overcome a grudge, reducing prospects of resolution even further. Attempts to reach out to them can go amiss, since even acts of kindness or gestures of support can be misconstrued as having malevolent intentions. Such individuals also irritate colleagues because of their constant need for reassurance and their never-ending dramas. Colleagues frequently become bored or frustrated, resulting in the person's rejection – and thereby their fears again become a self-fulfilling prophecy.

The primary defence mechanism of the paranoid is splitting, where they divide the world into either friends or enemies. Such rigid thinking means they are unlikely to change their view. If you are on the receiving end of such individuals, the best response is to hold firm to reality and inhibit any tendency to rise to their bait. Keep the emotional temperature down by speaking in a direct, yet firm, matter-of-fact tone. It is your tone rather than your words that will come across. Be careful not to become the adversarial person he or she imagines you to be. Recognise that logic and reason may not penetrate and accept there are limits as to what you can get across.

Paranoid people often take refuge in perfectionism. Fear of being humiliated means they go to extreme lengths to avoid making mistakes. Imagined mistakes can feel as real as actual ones.

Another favoured defence mechanism is projection – perceiving one's negative traits in another person as a way of shedding qualities despised in oneself. This can lead to dangerous misunderstandings, unfair blaming or even bullying of the person wrongly accused. The person who is projecting pressures the victim of his accusations to act in ways that show the unwanted traits lie with them and not the projector. The individual on the receiving end of projection can react by either accepting it and believing they are indeed inadequate – for example, if a paranoid manager repeatedly tells one of his team that he or she has done badly in a particular task, that person may come to believe it, become anxious, lose confidence and underperform as a result. The combined dynamics of the two individuals is referred to as 'projective identification' as the victim 'identifies' with what is being projected on to them. Alternatively, if they have the emotional maturity to know they are being wrongly accused, they will resist the projection and conflict is likely to erupt.

The way to protect yourself against unfair projection is to:

1. Recognise when accusations are unfair and belong with the other.
2. Recognise that another person is attempting to make you feel inadequate.
3. Decide firmly not to accept the projection and inhibit any tendency to act out the projected behaviour.

Projection, and those who are unable to resist it, incidentally, explain how paranoia and other emotions can become contagious in an organisation, as people instil their fears and anxieties into others in turn. If a company is performing badly and redundancies are rumoured, for instance, a worker insecure about his abilities and consequently in fear of losing his job can project this insecurity into others, who in turn might push it into other colleagues and so on in a domino effect. If a leader is paranoid he/she is likely to create a paranoid culture where fear runs rampant and, again, clashes are a likely result.

If you struggle with paranoia, here are some questions to ask yourself:

- In childhood, did you feel you could trust the people closest to you or not? Who were they?
- At work, do you believe you are being judged unfairly more often than not, and by whom?
- Do you think that people frequently dislike you?
- When you receive bad feedback, do you take it personally and think the person is against you?
- Do you often anticipate a negative response from others even though your experience provides evidence to the contrary?
- Are you likely to focus on a single rejection to an extent that other positive experiences are dismissed?

While being disliked or downtrodden is intolerable for most of us, attempting to flee from it by constantly seeking reassurance or projecting your feelings of inadequacy on to others will only make matters worse. Instead, explore your worries with an ally – preferably outside the organisation – where you can gain perspective and determine where reality lies.

The following case of George and his boss, Bill, encompasses much of what has been discussed in this chapter and provides a striking example of how combined feelings of inadequacy, rage, paranoia, envy and associated defence mechanisms can turn toxic.

George, a Welshman in his early forties, was appointed as communications director for an international company. His boss, Bill, had been promoted to an executive role but lacked the necessary skills for the job. With no talent for strategy, he hid behind process and detail and surrounded himself with 'yes' people to hide his limitations. In contrast, George was an experienced communications professional who had good interpersonal skills, high intelligence and could read a room well. He was liked and respected by colleagues and clients but nevertheless, his personality was on the dependent side. He suffered from insecurities, was eager to please and craved reassurance.

Over time, it became clear that Bill was envious of George's personable nature and his capacity to enthuse a room with innovative ideas and strategic plans. George's strong performance put Bill in a negative light, which infuriated him and his resulting destructive envy made George the obvious target on which to project his feelings of inadequacy. Through projective identification – setting unreasonable tasks and becoming highly critical – Bill attempted to rid himself of his inadequacies by undermining George.

George described how his boss had been pleasant initially, encouraging him to settle in slowly, but then quickly changed tack. Matters eventually came to a head when Bill was faced with a forthcoming international conference. He rang George in a panic, saying he had to come up with a brand strategy to present at the conference within two weeks, which, under extreme pressure, George managed to deliver.

'I should have said to myself there is no way in hell, considering the complexity, I could have done that,' George told me in my consulting room. 'I was so panicked by what was a totally schizophrenic response, from him being sweetness and light in the first weeks to being very aggressive and threatening, that I spent two weeks working 12-hour days writing a strategy and got it to him with the caveat that it needed some serious market testing.'

The idea was then to present his strategy first to the main board. But when he ran it by Bill, he received a panicked phone call before the board meeting warning him against presenting it.

'I thought to myself, either I have the courage of my conviction and present the strategy or I just reel out a bunch of tactical activity, which is what he had asked me to do. So I thought, bugger it, I'm going to present my strategy. Within five minutes the chief executive said, "This is good, I get it." People came up to me afterwards to say, "That was really inspiring." I said to [my boss], "How do you think that went?" and he said to me, in a crazy, sarcastic voice: "How do YOU feel that went?"

'I really bust a gut to produce high-quality work and what

I realised was that strategically he didn't get it. The way he operated was in a totally obsessive tactical mode which often mistook process for outcomes. In truth, he wasn't that bright – he was also deeply institutionalised having worked for the organisation for 30 years. Through a combination of sycophancy and workaholism he had managed to climb his way up but he wouldn't have survived ten minutes in another organisation.'

This was the beginning of a swift, brutal end to George's 18 months at the company, as he explained: 'The previous Friday, I'd given a really good presentation, lots of people were saying it was fantastic. On the next Monday, he called me into his room and said, "This is not working out, I'm going to give you this opportunity to resign and if not we're going to manage you out".'

George's dependent personality meant he had tended to overestimate his part in his deteriorating relationship with his boss and this had kept him in the job beyond the point where he should have left. His need for acceptance meant that he ignored the toxic nature of the company and instead pressed on, hoping for a better response.

'If somebody says something is not working my immediate response is to redouble my efforts to the point at which I get it right. Because the alternative is catastrophic – I lose this job. I'm not loved.'

George underwent this experience while in therapy with me. He had already told me that in his childhood his mother had often been cold and aloof. He had to work hard to gain a response from her that made him feel loved. Occasionally, she responded with warmth and this kept him craving more. So in our sessions, he came to see the link between his relationships with his mother and the one he had with his boss, and the fact that he could not give up on either. His dependent personality had led him to comply with Bill's harmful projections. The recognition that he was a target of his boss's projections and envious attacks was crucial in helping George through his departure and to recover quickly. He was able to leave successfully because he had rightfully located the 'unwanted traits' in Bill and not himself. With his confidence regained, he was able to go on to success elsewhere.

Whether conflicts arise as a result of envy, paranoia or excessive rage, it is often managers who eventually have to deal with them – or more accurately, the difficult individuals involved. Here are some tips for dealing with extreme personalities and paranoid individuals:

- Do not show anger or raise the emotional temperature. For people who cannot control their emotions, this is only likely to escalate matters rather than resolve them.
- For individuals who cannot tolerate negative feedback, praise when you can and try to reframe any criticism in a way that feels more bearable.
- Stick to procedures and avoid comments that may be interpreted as personal attacks.
- Ensure the psychological safety of staff and set clear boundaries – they will be closely observing how bad behaviour is dealt with.

- If the person is rigid do not try to convince them that their thinking is wrong, you will only get into a power struggle.
- Reframe the issue as a 'problem for us', or 'I find it difficult' rather than 'you are being difficult' in order to encourage a collaborative approach.

The fault may not always lie entirely with the individuals involved. Managers need to ask themselves if the organisation's culture breeds toxic behaviour, or even if their management style might unintentionally be creating an envious or paranoid environment. Leaders can improve matters by creating a climate of transparency. When managers make clear the reasons for their decisions, employees are less likely to allow their imaginations to create more sinister explanations. This is particularly the case for controversial ones regarding redundancies and restructuring. Remember also that excessive micromanaging can leave people believing they are being constantly judged and this can be interpreted as a threat rather than support.

It has to be stressed, however, that not all conflicts can be resolved and nor is it practical for organisations to go to the lengths of resolving particularly onerous ones. A cantankerous nightmare of an employee who causes unpleasant and unnecessary tensions might also be highly talented and make crucial contributions. In such cases, learning how best to manage the individual might be the sensible compromise for the overall good of the organisation.

This point is made vividly by Kerry Sulkowicz, the leading US psychoanalyst and adviser to corporate leaders. He advises managers that conflicts of a long duration may be indicative of something deeply embedded in the psyches of each individual and the dynamic they form.

'It can be a sado-masochistic dynamic – where one is constantly trying to get the other to submit and the other pushes back but then continuously puts themselves in harm's way and provokes the same kind of dominance-like behaviour,' he says.

In such cases, for many organisations the solution will be structural rather than psychological, he says, simply because there is neither the time nor resources to investigate the dynamics involved in more depth. Transferring an individual to another department or in some scenarios negotiating their departure may be the best solution to an insurmountable conflict.

'These deep-seated conflicts typically end with somebody leaving or at least changing roles ... it's worked out structurally rather than purely psychologically because it's a systemic issue – you're not dealing with one person in a vacuum.'

And he adds: 'When [managers'] rational approaches don't seem to help, one of my favourite things to say is, "Your problem is that you're too rational." Being rational is a good thing, yes, but it's actually crazy to think you can solve everything rationally – or that people are going to be acting rationally all the time and therefore will just respond to rational suggestions. That's actually irrational!'

7

# In fear of conflict – or, why there is no such thing as a perfect childhood

Stan had been a client of mine for a short while before he presented one particular issue that was troubling him. A debonair man in his early forties, he had initially come to see me because the tough decisions he had to make at work caused him extreme anxiety, to the point where he was experiencing panic attacks. When he worked independently as a software designer, he found work exciting and rewarding. But since starting his own successful software company, he had increasingly found the pressure of managing staff and making decisions that upset people unbearable. Consequently, he was unable to solve serious problems and take the business forward. Although he recognised his faults, the feelings were so extreme that he was unable to do what he knew was necessary for the company's survival.

On this particular day, he sat upright and began to talk. His confident persona faded and his tone softened as he spoke of interpersonal tensions in the business: 'I just lie awake all hours of the night worrying about having to talk to Angie,' he said.

Stan had begun his business in London more than ten years previously and eventually expanded by opening offices in continental Europe. Following his decision to have an office in Amsterdam, he took on a partner, Angie, a woman a little younger than him whom he had known personally and professionally for more than a decade. Although he was initially excited at the prospect of her running the Amsterdam office, it turned out she was not up to the job. During the first year she failed to meet targets and was costing the company a lot of money. Consequently, Stan decided to shut the branch and tell Angie she no longer had a role in the business. Yet however rational his decision, he could not bring himself to tell her. He would rehearse the conversation in his mind but the imagined scenario would make him panic and so he put it off.

'I imagine you're terrified of facing her anger towards you and your guilt at upsetting her,' I suggested. He nodded in recognition.

Stan is not unusual. Many of us are better equipped to handle a full-on crisis than to deal with awkward conversations that leave us feeling vulnerable. We may dread the guilt we feel when giving someone bad news or simply be unable to face the possibility of being disliked. Or we fear the conversation might lead to a confrontation that will leave us mentally paralysed and unable to think on our feet. Stan had hoped that by avoiding the conversation the problem would resolve itself. But of course, such magical thinking only perpetuated matters. Procrastinating had not only worsened his anxiety but also allowed time for the issue to become more complicated. During the time he delayed talking to Angie, she had become depressed. This only added to his guilt and meant that he postponed the conversation yet again. Matters deteriorated further when she announced she was pregnant.

At this point, he had begun to feel victimised by the situation, imagining that she had intentionally fallen pregnant to avoid being fired – an extreme reaction that indicated to me that there was more going on here than everyday aversion to conflict. He also worried that he might face accusations of sexual discrimination should he dismiss her. Stan was now ready to examine his fears and the unrealistic responsibility he felt towards Angie. He told me how as a child, he had been left to look after a single mother who suffered depression and often reacted aggressively towards him when he said anything that upset her. Thus, from an early age, he was convinced that saying anything difficult would only leave him with more to contend with rather than less.

'Perhaps subconsciously you fear the same aggressive reaction from Angie,' I said. 'By avoiding conversations with her you're attempting to distance yourself from childhood feelings.'

Again, he nodded in recognition.

In our subsequent sessions Stan was able to face these early experiences and separate his relationship with his mother (the past) from scenarios at work (the present). More importantly, he was able to see Angie for who she was and the potential harm to his business. Once the link was made, he was able to assert himself and tell Angie she had to leave. Some of his fears were realised, others not. Although she responded with rage and threats of legal action, he survived her anger without feeling guilty or responsible. If anything, he was resentful. And having shed those uncomfortable feelings, he was able to tackle the legal issues and practical problems that ensued.

Most importantly, he was able to cope with the emotions because they were no longer ignited by repressed feelings from the past. Ultimately, he was enormously relieved for having dealt with the matter. Not only has the business thrived since but his confidence grew as a result.

For many, it is the interpersonal conflicts and difficult conversations at work above all else that evoke fear and dread. Avoiding such conversations can also result in leaders losing the respect of their team and ultimately undermining their authority. Yet it is finding creative solutions to them that helps businesses thrive.

Stan's experience illustrates how work tensions are not only fraught with interpersonal conflicts but internal ones as well. While he recognised it was crucial for the business that Angie leave, he also feared the potential fallout. Often such internal conflicts, above and beyond the interpersonal ones, stop people in their tracks.

The mind has many ways to defend against a fear of conflict. Denial, or refusing to acknowledge the problem exists, is the most dangerous defence. Avoidance is the most common. Fear of the situation is often the overriding feeling and this can stymie thinking so that nothing gets done. The longer one procrastinates, the bigger the issue tends to grow in one's mind until the imagined scenario has outgrown the actual one and eventually seems too big to confront.

Brushing aside or minimising the issue, or changing the subject are other approaches that are just as problematic. The wish that it would go away becomes the prevalent thought as the issue continues to be kicked down the road. An illusion sets in that the conflict will vanish without any action being required.

Our present politically correct culture is more conflict averse, and while this creates better behaviour, it risks driving disputes under cover and becoming more covert. Having to carefully monitor your language is a useful skill but becoming too cautious can muddle what you have to say or be construed as being apologetic.

In our world of 'safe spaces', 'no platforming' and 'cancel culture', an underlying belief has emerged that the workplace should protect people from being upset. But taken to an extreme, the attitude undermines the need to prepare individuals for the inevitable blows, disappointments and frustrations work provokes. Rather than building resilience and strengthening their emotional muscle, people sidestep bad feelings. I am not arguing against protecting individuals from bullying, harassment and unfair treatment. Strong feelings, however, are an inevitable reality of working life and those better equipped to deal with them will be more successful and enable organisations to run more efficiently.

Few of us are immune from a dread of conflicts – even powerful leaders. Many rise to their positions because of their unique skills, expertise and experience, rather than their interpersonal abilities in facing the strong emotions provoked when presenting bad news or unpopular decisions. Once at the top, many avoid difficult conversations. They recoil from their fear, guilt and embarrassment as well as the shock, hurt and hostility they anticipate will be directed at them. With promotion comes more decisions to take and with that more people to disappoint or anger. It is no wonder many leaders run for cover. But the best executives face such challenges – and this is what convinces staff of their ability to lead.

At a lower level, the prospect of giving bad feedback or warnings to an employee can make a manager panic before the conversation has begun. The unpredictability of how the discussion might unfold nags away at them. The longer the wait, the more catastrophic the imagined outcome grows in one's mind.

Making staff redundant is no doubt the most gruelling conversation to be had. One founder of a start-up put it to me this way: 'I didn't get into [business] to mess up people's careers – it's absolutely not what I'm there for. And being made to feel that I'm doing something wrong, even though, objectively, it's my company and I decide who works there and who doesn't, within boundaries.'

He reached a point where he felt victimised by the staff member he wished to make redundant even though he was damaging the business by his incompetence.

'I would hope that he wouldn't be in the office, I didn't want to be near him. Then I felt like a crazy person. This is my business, I'm employing people – how am I in a situation where I'm spending all this money on an office and hiding from them? It was part of the realisation of what I needed to do.'

He later found reading the vitriolic emails from the person he had made redundant the most excruciating part.

'I felt I had to absorb all of that. Then negotiations over redundancy pay took over every waking second. I wasn't prepared for that draining period where you're just having to seal the deal. And meanwhile the rest of the team were looking at me like, "You're the bad person, you sacked our friend". Then I had to give an account to everyone. I cried – which I now think massively helped the PR effort because it showed that I wasn't a monster.

'It wasn't until a few days later that I had a sense of relief. It wasn't as bad as my fears. I'd had this long period of dread and actually it wasn't as bad as the dread I felt. The business was a lot happier without him. I was certainly happier without him. It was the right decision. I wish I would have done it sooner. I would definitely be less scared of doing it again.'

The relief this entrepreneur felt is typical – many managers find it empowering to have faced such conversations and seen the benefits of making tough decisions. Although many people kid themselves that confronting conflicts will make matters worse and so brush them aside, in reality they do not disappear but re-emerge in ways that are often more destructive and difficult to spot. Staff involved can retaliate with malicious gossip, poor productivity and foster a loss of motivation among colleagues.

When leaders and managers avoid difficult conversations they create cultures which discourage staff from raising such issues. Elizabeth Wolfe Morrison and Frances J. Milliken coined the phrase 'organisational silence' to describe the phenomenon of employees withholding their concerns for fear their opinions will be dismissed or incur repercussions. Wolfe Morrison and Milliken add that leaders of fear-ridden organisations typically avoid information that makes them feel weak, incompetent or embarrassed, and respond by ignoring, dismissing or attacking its credibility. As a result, they fail to benefit from the diverse ideas and depth of talent in their teams.

Leaders at organisations such as these might believe employees are self-interested and untrustworthy, or simply that managers know best. They think agreement and consensus signify organisational health, dissent and disagreement the opposite. Because staff are regarded as hostile opponents or apathetic observers, the highly centralised decision making excludes employees. As a result upward communication is discouraged and managers are left in the dark. But innovation requires that people feel able to challenge beliefs and, more importantly, to fail. When disagreement and mistakes are discouraged, companies risk undermining the very inventiveness they need to grow. Creatives will become frustrated and leave, and if a company is seen to have a revolving-door syndrome it will have more difficulty in attracting talented staff.

Steven knows all this too well because he works in a creative industry. He recognises the need for staff to express themselves and that creative freedom can potentially lead to disagreements and even conflicts. We discussed this on the phone during the 2020 pandemic lockdown.

He had worked in advertising for more than 25 years and was currently managing director of his branch. Yet while confident about making tough decisions, and even fighting his corner when it involved issues he felt competent about, conversations regarding staff's performance and behaviour left him highly anxious to the extent his heart raced and muscles tensed; the fear was excruciating and he went to extreme lengths to avoid it. He would rather delegate the task, dodge the issue, write an email – anything, in fact, not to face the conversation head on.

Steven is highly sensitive and easily emotionally swayed. His sensitivity drew out many of his strengths, such as his creativity, wide-ranging interests, deep empathy and intense emotional awareness. With good early family experiences, highly sensitive people like him can flourish – but there is a challenging side. At times he was overwhelmed physically, mentally and emotionally by personal tensions at work. If someone else was upset, he felt it, too.

Before entering management he had relied on his talent, intelligence and charm to achieve results both in his education and career. He was often praised and admired, and this confirmed a preferred view of himself and kept his negative traits under wraps. But when he began dealing with disgruntled staff who were angry at him for challenging their performance, his tightly guarded sense of self unravelled.

'Sometimes I wonder if I did the wrong thing [by becoming a manager] – should I have stuck with the "craftmanship", which I enjoyed 100 per cent?' he said he often asked himself. 'I was really carefree by comparison as it didn't carry this human stress.'

He sounded frustrated, even angry, so I asked: 'Do you find yourself irritated much of the time?' I wondered if he was angry with staff for making him feel a bad person.

'I do find [dealing with difficult people] upsetting, frustrating and boring and my general feeling is "Why not just drop it, why does it matter so much to you?" Irritating is right. And it takes up a lot of time. It is by far the biggest thing I have to deal with. I do think it holds me back. If it's about working on an account they don't want to, as a manager, I'm perfectly entitled to ask them [to do it]. But if I think somebody has not worked hard enough, I find those performance conversations upsetting and I shy away from them. I'll think about the conversation before and after – it will play on my mind.'

'Can you give me an example?' I asked.

'I've had frequent conversations with a low performer but nothing has changed. I don't think she realises just how badly regarded she is. I find that conversation hard to have, [telling her] "You really need to up your game." We even went through a performance review process and I found the whole thing excruciating.'

'Why do you think these conversations go wrong?' I asked.

'I say things in such a neutral or understated way that the person doesn't get the message I'm trying to convey.'

When he observed the more aggressive approach of some of his colleagues, he decided their approach gained no better results and so he reverted to type, justifying his style. 'My old boss, people don't tell her things because they think they're going to upset her and she'll go into a rage. It's a bad position to be in as a boss when people aren't telling you what's going on. I think it's worse than being too soft.'

Another one of his tactics was stressing the positive. 'One of my 360 degree reports said, "He wants to ignore bad news." I try and say, "That's a great thing you've done but this issue needs to be addressed as well."'

'What is it you fear?' I asked.

'I don't want people to think badly of me. Even though there is no reason why I should be worried as I don't think they would. But subconsciously, I have this concern.'

He worried that others may see him as mean, unfair or aggressive, leaving him feeling ashamed and horrible about himself.

'Underlying it,' I suggested, 'is a dread of strong feelings. Both yours and theirs. Perhaps it's painful imagining that you could be seen as a bad guy. But wanting to be seen as the good guy runs counter to the need to be aggressive in order to make tough and sometimes, unpopular decisions.'

'Yes, that's right – I don't like it. I normally think through those conversations quite a lot and then I pretend to be somebody else. I think how they would do it. I adopt a persona. I find my voice changing – it goes very low and I don't sound like my normal self.'

I asked Steven about his early life. He described both parents as attentive, caring and loving, insisting there was nothing dysfunctional. His older brother was more argumentative and frequently in conflict with their parents, but early on Steven decided that was not for him. So he became the peacemaker in the family.

'It seems you've taken on the same role with your team,' I said. 'Confronting staff on their performance is not what peacemakers do.'

His sensitivity is ingrained in his character. Fortunately, the good nurturing from his family helped him use his sensitivity to his advantage. His parents generally reinforced what an intelligent, likeable and talented person he was. Throughout his education and career, he continued to build on the excellent feedback he received and this led him to develop a strong and positive sense of himself. Eventually, however, he discovered that the world does not always reflect the same wonderfulness. When faced with someone upset by *his* feedback, a chink in his armour was exposed.

The difficulty in aspirational families such as Steven's where children are highly praised is that the child is encouraged to believe the hype – that everything about them is brilliant. It's yet another example of the law of unintended consequences; specifically, that positive parenting and a nurturing childhood environment does not necessarily make one immune from anxieties further down the line. While this boosts their self-worth, confidence and later their career advancement, conflicts at work can be a blow to their self-esteem when they are unexpectedly cast as aggressive, unfair or 'a bad person.'

While being the adored son or daughter has advantages, psychoanalyst and writer Adam Phillips believes it is not necessarily all plain sailing.

'It might leave you with a sense of specialness that the world does not mirror back to you, giving you a grandiose sense of yourself and with a disappointment in the world,' he told me. 'The person may become outraged when people don't take them on their own terms. It is as if mothers have said, "You are already perfect" – then there's nothing left to do. It pre-empts their development, as if nothing has to be earned. What you're left with then is a false sense of entitlement.'

As Steven's story demonstrates, there is no guarantee that a good attachment experience will lead to a life free of internal conflicts and anxiety. This prompts a necessary warning to readers. Blame for many of the demons, psychological traits, fears and anxieties I have discussed so far has been laid at the door of our early lives, or specifically at poor parenting. Yet even the best, most concerned parenting can leave one ill-equipped to deal with many challenges in the workplace. Raising children is no easy business. It may be time to let your parents off the hook and just make the best of your upbringing.

Psychotherapists have a useful term to help ease the pressure on parents who feel the need to be perfect: they need only be 'good enough,' a phrase coined in 1953 by Donald Winnicott, a British paediatrician and psychoanalyst who was hugely influential in the field of developmental psychology. He suggested mothers need only provide the right environment for children to thrive. This means allowing themselves to have imperfections while supporting their children through their anxieties and rages to help them cope with life's realities. Children, he suggests, can actually benefit when their parents fail them in manageable ways. The frustrations, disappointments and irritations that are bound to arise can help children learn to cope with such occurrences later in life.

So delving into one's inner and early life need not necessarily imply blame or fault with one's parents. My intention is to encourage you to think, to wonder, to examine – to arrive at hypotheses to be considered if useful and then put aside when further ideas come to mind. Remember that reflections need only lead to further understanding rather than an absolute truth. If we become too committed to our explanations we cease thinking and considering further possibilities. Our families and early lives certainly play a significant part in our development and an underestimated one in the arena of work. However, our generational history, genetics, class, culture, socio-economic factors – and luck – all contribute. Making sense of how we tick is a complex and complicated process and one that leaves some questions unanswered. It is the journey, rather than arriving at a specific destination, that helps us develop our understanding of ourselves. Yes, the 'Aha!' moments of insight surprise and inspire us but self-examination is a continuous, lifelong process.

Jens Stoltenberg, who became prime minster of his native Norway and later secretary general of NATO, knows all too well how one's path in life can be a mystery. In 2020, he talked to the BBC about the death of his younger sister in her early fifties as a result of drug addiction, a tragedy that left him with unanswered questions.

He said: 'For me, it will always be a paradox and something I will never be able to explain: why, in a family with three children, my bigger sister Camilla ends up as a medical doctor – she is now director of the Norwegian public health agency. I end up prime minister and secretary general of NATO – and then my little sister, growing up in the same room as I did, in the same street with the same friends, attending the same school – she ends up a drug addict and passes away much too early.'

In my early years as a family therapist, I specialised in helping those with a family member who suffered from an eating disorder. They were often referred by a psychiatrist, who would eagerly await my conclusions as to why an otherwise normal young girl would choose to starve herself. Often, however, I disappointed. The families I saw impressed me with their courage, strength and willingness to take responsibility. Often they blamed themselves, thinking their child's illness was punishment for their failure as parents. But I saw a different story: a family struck by an inexplicable tragedy. Yes, if I dug deeply enough, I could arrive at a hypothesis that might satisfy the family and the medical team. Yet in the main I saw a loving and caring unit. Parents are not perfect, none of us are. Yes, there might have been room for psychological growth, but there was generally little to indicate why their child had become so severely ill. Furthermore, even if the family presented as dysfunctional, there was always the possibility this resulted from living with an eating disorder and not the other way around. Much of my time was spent trying to relieve parents of their guilt, which was neither appropriate nor useful. The best approach was to try to understand the problem the child herself was trying to solve or emotions she was attempting to express through her symptoms and body size. Was she trying to encourage more family unity or communicate needs she dare not voice? There would be multiple understandings and meanings unique to each family.

If you are someone who routinely avoids conflict, ask yourself the following questions to determine your underlying motivations:

- Do you fear being disliked or seen as the 'bad one'?
- Do you worry your reputation will be harmed or dwell on what might happen should things go badly wrong?

- Are you lost for words or paralysed in the moment?
- Do you dread strong feelings such as guilt, anger and humiliation?

You might tick several or even all of these boxes. Now look at your answers and consider if you have other motivations for avoiding conflict. Reflect on your early family life for more clues.

A leader who wishes to avoid conflict may employ a range of techniques – which can be effective in sidestepping dealing with an issue directly but ultimately damaging to the organisation. One way a senior leader may do this is by surrounding themselves with 'yes' people who are unlikely to disagree. This creates an echo chamber where employees tell their superiors only what they want to hear, with the obvious danger being that the top person becomes immune from hearing important information.

A manager with a fear of conflict might delegate difficult conversations with their staff to the human resources department or a coach. They hope, for example, that a good coach will be able to turn an underachieving employee's performance around and save them from having to confront the problem. Loyal deputies may also be roped in as a proxy or buffer. One senior manager described to me how his boss made him the 'bad cop.'

'I [used to] have to be the confrontational one,' he told me. 'But these days I tell him, "No, you need to do this. You're the president of the bank."'

Some leaders of multinational organisations make themselves invisible, travelling excessively and rarely touching down. Fearing that conversations could turn out badly, they literally and figuratively keep to the skies. They might even feel victimised by the very situation they should be managing. Instead of having clear, direct and responsible conversations, they panic. They think if the person who is underperforming, for example, would only do their job they would not have to summon the energy to confront them.

But whatever the avoidance technique, those who take a totally passive stance do so usually because they fear making matters worse and therefore they keep their concerns to themselves. The danger of this is twofold. One is that the issue is never dealt with, left to fester and grows out of control. The other is that their resentments build inside them until they can no longer be contained. Eventually they explode in frustration and rage inappropriately, causing even more confusion and a bigger mess. Then, seeing the damage they have done, they feel ashamed or guilty, or both, and determine to never risk being confrontational again. Typically, however, the cycle repeats itself because the root of the problem is not addressed.

Many people lack basic assertion skills and find themselves lost for words. They might attempt to 'cushion the blow' by choosing their words too carefully. Their soft tone and smiles are in contrast to their harsh words and this undermines any prospect of the message being received clearly. Or they smother the bad news between layers of positive comments, their meaning lost in an upbeat torrent. They end up only muddling their message and confusing their listeners by failing to be clear.

Assertion does not come naturally to most people. Rather it is an acquired skill. It is commonly confused with aggression but there is a significant difference. Aggression involves getting your view across but with little or no regard for the person receiving them. However, when the other person feels attacked, disregarded or not given an opportunity to respond, they are likely to shut down and there is little chance that the message will penetrate. They are also more likely to respond in turn, often passively through reducing their productivity, silently withdrawing or even secret sabotage.

Assertion is about communicating respectfully. Assertive people are mindful of their tone and language, and remain interested in the other's thoughts and feelings. They also know a conversation can be unpredictable and so they allow for flexibility. The good news is that assertion techniques can be learnt easily, much more so than tackling some of the deeper psychological issues described in this book. The techniques below may feel unnatural initially, but with practice and the satisfaction of getting your points across you are likely to improve quickly.

Here are some do's and don'ts when handling difficult conversations.

**Do:**

- Act quickly. Do not wait for the issue to resolve itself.
- Be prepared – think through the conversation and possible scenarios.

- Clearly state the purpose of the conversation.
- Keep your tone neutral. Tone weighs heavier than words.
- Make your language clear and direct.
- Stick to the point and repeat yourself if necessary.
- Ensure your words match your tone and expression.
- Stay curious about the other's thoughts and feelings.
- Ask questions.
- State areas where you agree or disagree.
- Allow time for the other person to respond.

**Don't:**

- Have too many assumptions about what will happen.
- Overstate or minimise the problem.
- Say too much or muddle your words.
- Be defensive or interrupt what the other person is saying.
- Try to smooth things over.
- Complicate matters by bringing in other issues.
- Try to lighten a serious conversation by smiling.
- Take the conversation personally.

Another avoidance technique is creating an overly optimistic culture where solutions are given priority and bad news regarded with disdain. While optimism is a commendable trait and organisations are more likely to excel in such an atmosphere as opposed to a pessimistic one, there are dangers when a positive bias makes it difficult for staff to report negative news. 'Bring me your solutions and not your problems,' is the cry of the highly anxious leader who fears discord and dissent. Employees are thereby conflicted – if they bring bad news they feel guilty about upsetting the apple cart but if they do not problems remain unsolved. They are also left holding the unpleasant information in their minds, while their boss continues to bask in illusion. Furthermore, such a culture makes it difficult for staff to ask for help. After all, if everything is running smoothly, why should you need it?

Optimistic cultures can thrive only when optimism is based on evidence. When it is used as a veil, it makes people anxious because realities are ignored. It is the manager's role to create an atmosphere where individuals are free to be productive, creative and free from worry about problems their managers are unwilling to face. Overstating the positive will also repel some clients. Intelligent people see through such facades and are not impressed. Experienced business people want to hear the truth; they know that avoiding uncomfortable realities leads only to stagnation or worse.

If ever there was a purveyor of optimism at work, it was Alice. She joined a small media company in her early thirties and brought with her a tenet of her working philosophy: creating an optimistic mood in which people could flourish. In previous jobs she had thrived on being the 'big shot' – inspiring colleagues, responding to challenges and creating new opportunities. It was the emotional nourishment from inspiring colleagues, rather than recognition from authority figures, that she craved.

'At most of the organisations I've worked for, I'd been able to build a strong peer group who absolutely believed in me

100 per cent. It's about us doing something because we're inspired to do it, and I'm at the centre of that.'

Being admired by colleagues and, more crucially, creating a positive and upbeat atmosphere, lifted her mood. Being at the centre of a close-knit team gave her security. However, there were costs – both to her, colleagues and the companies she worked for. While she remained highly regarded, others whom she deemed not as sharp as her would be left out. In addition, maintaining an overly optimistic atmosphere made it difficult to give negative feedback.

'If I know I'm going to have a difficult conversation, I anticipate and worry, and my heart is pounding. It's hard because I want the dynamic to be positive and one that's moving forward. I dread having to say, "Actually, you're not living up to your objectives."'

When she had a baby, however, lack of sleep, having to juggle childcare and a new role, left her drained, lost and empty. 'I felt I was failing or letting people down,' she told me. 'I could see 25 things that I'd not done and worried that I wasn't living up to my potential.'

Alice was exhausted from inspiring and energising people all the time. The repressed bad feelings and worries were taking a toll. Secretly, she longed for help. 'Do you ever just wish there was a grown-up to hand things off to? In a small business, you're making it up as you go along. When things get too much, you think, "Jesus, how can there not be someone with more experience and knowledge to help me?"'

I was curious about where her dread of bad feelings came from.

Alice recounted her family story, where there was much to be gained from a sense of safety and belonging. The price, however, was that everyone was expected to sing the same tune, and differences and strong feelings were discouraged. She was the eldest of three siblings in a strong, close-knit family where Christian values were emphasised and she felt a responsibility to adhere to norms. Her family created a sense of being special and different, and the strict Christian beliefs enhanced the notion of there being a 'correct' way to behave. Both she and her brother were 'effortlessly academically brilliant' and that became part of the family narrative.

'The family dynamics fostered this belief that you're either in or out,' she explained, 'and being part of the family involved being gifted.'

As a teenager, she did things that infuriated her parents – drinking too much and having a boyfriend – and this left her feeling unacceptable. 'The amount of panic I felt over minor infractions, like smoking, was disproportionate to the actual gravity of the crime because it felt that nobody would ever love me anymore,' she explained.

'One of the responsibilities I take is not to express my negative emotions,' she added. 'Even though you feel sad, you should pretend to feel happy because that's how you make everyone else around you happy.'

Her parents were intolerant of negative emotions and she found herself resorting to destructive ways, such as self-harming, to release pent-up rage, sadness and frustration. Later, achievement at work replaced harmful strategies for fending off unbearable feelings.

'Can you say more about how your work resembles your early family life?' I asked

'That feeling of being at the centre of things, of everyone agreeing this is an exciting thing we're all going to do together, that feels an attempt to recapture a family culture that felt very secure – it's definitely a happy place.'

For Alice, an optimistic environment gave her a sense of belonging, acceptance and even love. Disagreements and disputes, she believed, could undermine the security she craved. The possibility that she could be ousted from her family for minor infractions motivated her to maintain an upbeat and optimistic culture in the workplace.

Family businesses are also notorious for avoiding conflicts. In my experience, they even shy away from meetings. There is an underlying assumption that if one issue is brought to the table, it might ignite a well of unresolved disputes going back years. It is easier by far to avoid difficult conversations all together. Disentangling historic family frictions from current business conflicts is not always obvious or easy. Unresolved early conflicts play themselves out at work and this makes it difficult to separate good business decisions from emotionally driven ones. For example, someone in the family who is seen as inadequate and unlikely to succeed elsewhere is given a role in the business with little or no qualifications.

People are able to bear harsh truths when they are fair and communicated in a non-confrontational yet direct way. Managers are often positively surprised by the result of being straightforward with difficult news. Most people can tolerate what is real. It is the covering up, equivocation or blatant avoiding of truths that causes more confusion and disturbance.

And remember that by avoiding difficult conversations you can end up harming yourself. When frustrations and resentments are repressed, the mind can convert them into self-critical thoughts. Withholding your views can make you doubt your own opinions, damaging your critical ability and sense of self-worth.

As one man said to me: 'You start to doubt whether your perception is the right one and begin to doubt yourself – you don't have a strong enough sense of self to say to yourself that you are right. It's a very confusing and unstable place to be.

'The realisation that you're doing this for security is shocking because you end up not being secure in yourself – and that is far more threatening to you than not being accepted by somebody else.'

# 8

# Control freaks, bullies and tyrants – how to deal with them and know when to run

Danny's dress sense is decidedly distant from the formal attire of business chic. The young, bearded entrepreneur's casual, even scruffy appearance illustrates that his focus is on his mind rather than body – more a neck-up than a neck-down kind of guy. His honesty and articulacy are part of an endearing personality that means he connects with people easily. He holds little back in our sessions, which makes for stimulating conversations.

Danny launched a technology start-up nearly a decade ago as a one-man show, relying on his knowledge, skills and contacts to establish it. As the business grew quickly, however, he was unprepared for the complications of bringing people in to meet its expanding demands. This was part of what brought him to me in the first place during those early years. In particular, he had been struck by a realisation.

'It was accepting that it was going to be either me doing it all – which wouldn't have been sustainable – or learning to delegate,' he told me then. 'This was made hard by being constantly let down [early on] by incompetents – liars and charlatans – people who were absolutely cavalier. I felt it was so much easier to do it myself than someone doing a bad job and me being cross about it.'

He explained that it also took him a while to understand that people were never going to share his intense belief in and passion for the business.

I told him: 'You worried they'll never live up to your standards – that they won't be you. And relying on people inevitably leaves you disappointed from time to time, creating more bad feelings.'

He agreed. 'I felt annoyed because I knew how to do all their jobs better than they could. So when they got it wrong I felt resentful that they couldn't just do it how I would like. When they asked me questions, I thought to myself, "Why can't they just figure it out?" That's not reasonable [on my part].'

A few years on and many sessions later, Danny and I discussed how he had been forced to confront what he had been – a 'control freak.' We reflected on how he had liked to think he trusted people but did not. He had regarded himself as self-sufficient, relying on his quick mind, focused attention and personality to succeed. Yet he had been forced to rein in his perfectionism and tendency to micromanage because otherwise the business would have been doomed.

'If I had stayed by myself without bringing in other people I would not have been able to live up to the standards I set for myself,' he said. 'As [the business] grew it would have become more impossible.'

He also remembered, contrarily, feeling threatened when an employee performed excellently. Fortunately, he had the maturity and insight to recognise his contradictions and was willing to change. 'This whole thing is supposed to be dependent on you and suddenly there's all these good people doing things. That's uncomfortable but also a powerful indicator that it isn't all about you.'

As a perfectionist he had feared that any shortcoming would lead to the business collapsing. The company felt an extension of himself and every mistake his personal failing. The consequent worry and attention to detail was exhausting, however, and he had come close to burnout. While any one of us with his level of ambition and responsibility would have found this challenging, for Danny, the need to control everything was so extreme as to risk destroying the business and his own health in the process. It had become apparent that underlying his control issues was an inability to tolerate uncertainty and a lack of trust in people that originated deep in his childhood.

'Unpredictability . . . is particularly worrying for me because it was such a theme of my upbringing,' he reflected.

From an early age Danny had attempted to control his immediate environment because it protected him from a home life that was full of chaos and confusion. His mother was an alcoholic, whose repeated admissions to rehabilitation facilities had little success. Meanwhile, his father was in denial of the damage his wife's drinking caused the family. Unable to trust that his parents could care for him, or even face the reality of his mother's addiction, left Danny fearing the worst.

'My big worry is me repeating this at work and becoming my unpredictable parents,' he said. 'Where everyone is left unable to know how to deliver baseline job performance, let alone succeed.'

He had transferred his internalised family on to his staff, fearing that the people he depended on for his livelihood could let him down with serious consequences. His behaviour was also an attempt to repress the hostility he had towards his parents, which he then directed towards his team, I suggested: 'While you complain about staff making huge errors of judgement, the people who actually put you at risk by their poor judgement were your parents.'

'I think that's right,' he replied. 'It's a similar feeling when you're let down by colleagues as being let down by family. You feel like you should be able to trust these people but then you can't and it's infuriating. It feels like an injustice – if there are people you pay to do the job and they don't do it, it's kind of inexplicable.'

He came to a realisation that his perfectionism had not only been a wish to control outcomes but also a means to silence an endless, self-abusing monologue in his mind. 'I was on myself to be perfect in a way that wasn't reasonable. Setting impossible targets and then abusing myself, telling myself I wasn't working hard enough, that I was useless, lazy, stupid and a loser all the time. Once I understood what I was doing, I literally stopped pretty much overnight.'

He said he had struggled with the tension created by having a perfectionist view of what was possible and the reality of life, and accepting that there was always going to be a gap between them. To release total control he had to tolerate the resulting uncertainty and anxiety, accepting that some employees might fall below his standards, while others might outperform him.

'Before, the problems in that gap would stack on top of

each other until it felt like you're carrying this backpack of all these mistakes physically weighing you down, whereas now they just happen and they pass and I get over it very quickly,' he said. 'Learning these things means you can make more mature decisions about the business and be less driven by emotion.

'Things are not going to work out in a way that you can control or predict. I found that difficult with the pandemic; the uncertainty being so huge that you couldn't control events. But I've learnt to relax into that space of the perfect and the possible. I stopped being deeply upset when I saw things that were not up to my standards. Through our conversations I was able to break that chain and now only become upset when people are seriously incompetent or commit grievous mistakes. Now the business feels closer to the job I do, rather than this extension of me that I'm trying to make perfect.'

Control freakery, the obsessive need to control one's environment, is particularly common among entrepreneurs such as Danny. The strong identification many have with their business propels them to control every aspect of it precisely because it feels so personal. They believe their business is about them entirely – their expertise, talents and connections they have made. Many fear that delegating would risk losing clients or the business failing. Lack of faith in their staff and their judgemental attitude fuels a compulsion to involve themselves in so many details that they lose sight of the bigger picture. Believing their way is the only way, they tend to hire people who replicate them rather than broadening the company's talents. Beliefs such as 'no one can do it as well as me' and 'people are bound to let me down' are typical justifications to keep a firm grip on events.

Even with a willingness to delegate, many new managers and founders are understandably confused as to how much autonomy and responsibility they can reasonably hand to staff. A typical pattern is oscillating between overly intruding into people's work and the opposite extreme, granting a free hand. Because micromanaging has received much negative press, they will tend to step back and hope for the best. Yet when a subsequent poor outcome confirms their fears, they revert to controlling behaviour.

The general assumption about micromanagement is that it is a batch of bad behaviours – such as interfering in people's work, not allowing individuals to think for themselves and creating unnecessary tension and anxiety in the workplace. But to suggest that micromanaging is entirely negative is neither useful nor accurate – much depends on the context and how it is perceived by the person on the receiving end. If one is newly employed and assigned a project, for example, hands-on advice and direction might be welcome. In another context, perhaps in a creative industry, similar direction might feel intrusive and irritating. When 'micromanaging' becomes the sole explanation for problems in the workplace, other contributing factors may be conveniently ignored. Someone who does not like to take orders, for example, might perceive feedback as micromanagement and dismiss crucial information.

Roshni Raveendhran is assistant professor at the Darden Graduate School of Business, University of Virginia. She has researched micromanaging extensively and concludes that it is best understood in terms of how a manager's behaviour is perceived by staff, rather than labelling it 'toxic.'

She explains: 'The exact same manager may be engaging in the same behaviour and while one person may perceive as it as micromanagement because it is inappropriate for the context they are working in, another person may perceive it as "this is helpful instruction" or "this will help me do a good job".'

She suggests leaders should learn to appreciate the nuances of what their staff can and cannot actually achieve and how their advice is perceived by others. Managers should not only pay attention to the feedback and subtle signals they receive from employees, but have honest and continuous conversations about how the work is going and how they can best support their staff. Many fail to appreciate that individuals have their unique ways of approaching work and perceiving support. While it is common practice to allow an orientation period for new staff to learn about a company, there is often no recognition that time is also needed for managers to get to know new employees.

The headline here is that leaders need to be curious, not just about employees' work experience and skills, but about who they are as people, what motivates, interests and excites them. Such conversations offer an opportunity to bring out the best in their team. Do they relish freedom and responsibility or do they work best with clear instructions and feedback? Finding out more about each member of your team will pay off handsomely.

As a manager, the onus is on you to set reasonable expectations and be confident the person you have delegated to is competent to do the job. This is a gradual process of handing over autonomy and responsibility while continuing to support and check in with staff. Once trust has been established on both sides, you can disengage and allow the freedom and autonomy so many people seek at work. There needs to be some allowance for failure because it is always a possibility and a willingness on both sides to learn from mistakes. As Bill Gates said: 'Success is a lousy teacher. It seduces smart people into thinking they can't lose.'

If you are convinced your team cannot be trusted, here are some tell-tale signs that the problem might lie with you:

- You are unable to see the bigger picture because your mind is cluttered with details.
- You think you alone are responsible for solving all the business's problems.
- You take credit for successes and blame for all failures.
- When the business fails to thrive, your response is to become more controlling.
- You feel overburdened with responsibility.
- Relationships at home are disrupted because you cannot switch off from work.
- You have difficulty asking for help.
- Staff stop bringing you their ideas and concerns because they find you unapproachable.
- You cannot believe others can do the job as well as you.
- You treat everyone the same, implying that you have failed to recognise the unique differences in your team.
- There is a high turnover of staff.

If you recognise yourself in most of these statements, you have a problem with control. Begin by examining yourself and pay attention to how your employees respond to you. If you accept that some of your behaviour is obstructing rather than enhancing your business objectives, then you can probably change and adopt fresh approaches to leadership. If, however, you find that delegating leaves you more anxious to the extent you are unable to release control, change may be more difficult because your underlying motivations are likely to be unconscious.

Control freakery stretches over a broad spectrum that begins with helpful attributes, such as drive, efficiency, attention to detail and a strong work ethic. At this healthier end, individuals are disciplined, organised and highly conscientious and as a result are often promoted. But there is a limit to how far they can go. Once in a management role, the same traits that helped them advance can undermine their ability to lead. Not only can they obstruct innovation and growth though their perfectionism and controlling behaviour, they can also undermine their staff by denying them any autonomy.

These managers create inefficiency because their perfectionistic tendencies mean they double check everything, so work takes longer. Their fierce attention to detail means they are often picking holes in employees' work, raising staff anxiety and thereby increasing the likelihood of mistakes. Strict adherence to rules is often coupled with a lack of joy or sense of fun – aspects that make work worthwhile beyond financial necessities. As a consequence, staff might feel undervalued, frustrated, bored and angry. They might cease thinking for themselves and deprive the company of their imaginative input. When such managers feel threatened they are likely to become more anxious, and consequently more controlling. If others do attempt to express an opposing view or challenge an opinion, they are often met with an aggressive response.

Leadership primarily involves bringing out the best in others and learning to step aside and find satisfaction from your team's success. But for overly controlling managers, the thrill of making the deal or being rewarded for a job well done is almost addictive – and the idea of handing over praise and rewards to underlings comes as a blow and a loss. Suddenly their lack of self-awareness and poor interpersonal skills are exposed.

The extreme end of the spectrum is characterised by rigid and intolerant thinking, manipulation and sometimes bullying. Milder control freaks can be taught leadership and delegation but for those at the other extreme change is nearly impossible because they are unlikely to recognise a problem exists, let alone seek help. There are deeper motivations – letting go of control may give rise to feelings of helplessness, of being overwhelmed and unable to cope. It can also reignite early traumas. For some, control is a way of managing their internal state because they have no other way of dealing with strong feelings. It is not just the business they fear might collapse but their internal world, too.

The unconscious motivation behind such obsessive/compulsive behaviour is often a desire to rid oneself of anxiety. Many new managers and founders cannot tolerate the uncertainty that is inevitable in a fresh role or venture. What if the business fails? How will I be judged should things not go well? Will I be seen as incompetent, or even disliked? For some, these fears can become so consuming that control becomes essential. Being able to predict outcomes, they believe, can offer assurance they are thought of highly. It confirms their acceptability and even lovability.

Margaret Heffernan, a former chief executive of media companies, author of successful business books including *Wilful Blindness* and *Uncharted*, and a professor specialising in leadership at the University of Bath, goes further. She told me: 'They want to feel that what is uncertain in the world is taken care of perfectly by other people. So, what happens is anxiety gets passed along the hierarchy. If you have a boss who's very anxious and will dictate a fair amount, for example, then they will micromanage people who will micromanage people until it becomes a very anxious culture. The more you try to control people, the more you create the requirement in them to revolt in order to articulate their autonomy and their adulthood. Because they feel the need to control is fundamentally infantilising.'

Those unable to tolerate the inevitable uncertainties frequently revert to perfectionism and workaholism. Their sense of identity is so closely tied with their work that anything perceived as not meeting expectations is experienced as a personal failing and loss of identity – it is that powerful. What they fail to realise, however, is that those very attempts to control events undermine the success they hope to achieve. Business is dynamic and for these individuals change is frightening. As long as they can stick to Plan A they can cope, but once forced to switch to Plan B they unravel. It is not only a distrust of others they react against but also a deep distrust of life itself. These people 'think' rather than 'feel' and while this might make them efficient, it tends to inhibit intuition, imaginative thinking and creativity. Innovation requires leaping into the unknown, being willing to try and fail, and tolerating outcomes. It is here that the controlling person reaches their limit.

Extreme controlling personalities have the potential to cause severe damage to an organisation and lasting harm to individuals in it. Healthy, functioning teams rely on a diversity of talent and this can be undermined by a leader who does not allow for varying views and repeatedly hires people who think like them. Their controlling behaviour has as much to do with managing their fragile sense of themselves as it does with relieving their anxiety.

An intolerance of uncertainty, Professor Heffernan believes, underpins their behaviour: 'There are people who believe that the world is fundamentally deterministic, that the future is knowable and therefore with enough data they can know the future. And knowing the future is what will relieve their anxiety. And if they don't know the future they are stupid and helpless but if they do know it they are in control and have some supreme power. And the way to know it is to have all the data about every little thing about my organisation.

'What gets lost is the value of uncertainty, which I see as possibility, and the value of giving people time and space to explore that, because that's where new ideas come from.'

Professor David Tuckett, a psychoanalyst, and director of the Centre for the Study of Decision-Making Uncertainty at University College London, concurs. He believes the past is not our best teacher because the future is not necessarily at all like the past. This is not to suggest that we cannot apply our experiences to better equip us for responding to unforeseen occurrences, but that when we do so we need to accept that for many crucial things the future is certain to be different in unexpected ways.

Professor Tuckett told me: 'Taking uncertainty seriously means in a deep way accepting that you cannot know. When people retort that surely we know some things, which is true, it's usually a defensive reaction to leaving their comfort zone to face that they cannot know, and need to enquire much more carefully.'

He says we can respond in one of two ways to uncertainties. One is to try to control events and outcomes by eliminating – or mocking – doubts so as not to be made anxious by them. The other is to pause and try to understand what is happening. Indeed, he suggests the most optimal state of mind for dealing with future uncertainty is curiosity and openness to experiment; in other words, having an inquisitive approach that can lead to innovation and discovery.

He added: 'A new situation can create curiosity, which means you can move towards the situation so you can understand it, or [it can create] anxiety – and you run away. Anxiety is a signal. It tells you there is something going on, pay attention! Because we have various cognitive capacities, we don't have to run away, we can say, "Hang on, let's have a closer look at this."

'Cognition and feeling are interlinked, so trying to know something is only possible if you don't mind feeling [the consequences of] whatever it is you get to know. Because change is happening so quickly, people are responding with more and more defensive behaviour – which is making things worse.'

Extreme control freaks make everyone's life a misery. They are the bullies and the tyrants, those who constantly move the goalposts so people do not know where they stand or what is expected. They have to be at the centre of everything – setting the agenda, taking the decisions and dominating conversations. Those who do not live up to their standards are made to feel miserable, are fired or demoted. In response, those around them become hyper-cautious, knowing that what they say will be noted and perhaps used against them further down the road. As a result, staff are left second-guessing what their boss wants rather than developing their own way of working.

If you have an absolute need for control then launching a business is perhaps the wrong direction for you because start-ups are inherently saturated with uncertainty.

Professor Heffernan again: 'It's like saying I have a huge fear of heights, I'm going to be an airline pilot. Being in a management position means you have tremendous power over people and your power to harm them psychologically in the long term is enormous. As a consequence, your responsibility is enormous. If your need for control is so great that you dump all your anxiety on to others, perhaps you're in the wrong spot.'

A friend told me of her experience of working for such a person. He was the founder and head of a company that had been established largely on his expertise and strong work ethic. A self-confessed workaholic, he expected the same commitment and drive from staff.

My friend, his chief operating officer, described to me the

frustrations of working for him. 'If he sends you an email, he expects you to respond immediately. If I see he's ringing me [while on another call], I have to finish my conversation and pick up the phone to him. Because if I don't then I'll get four or five phone calls from him saying, "pick up, pick up".

'He says what he thinks he should say and then follows it with the exact opposite behaviour. There's no recognition that people may want to have a Sunday afternoon with their family. At the end of a leadership meeting, he'll go, "Look, it's been a mad week, thanks for your efforts, try and get some downtime over the weekend," and the next breath he'll say, "Ted – let's pick up on Sunday."'

My friend's boss dominates discussions and decisions and needs to be the first to know everything. His charismatic personality only adds to the confusion. With him, you are either in or out.

'You've got to play his game. If you're in his good books it's fabulous, and when you're not it's horrible; he makes you feel crap. That's how he tries to get stuff done – if a carrot isn't working he'll beat you with a stick. People go through cycles – you're in the White House one day and the dog house the next.'

If an employee fails to deliver, give the right response or display the right attitude, there is a price to pay.

'How do you survive?' I asked.

'Talk to him when he wants to talk, answer emails when you get them. Be at his beck and call 24/7, do what you said you're going to do and life will be a lot easier.'

Many like him are successful precisely because of their workaholic habits. They are often better at managing up than managing down and because they do achieve results it means their bad behaviour is often overlooked by the powers that be.

Such controlling workaholics have obsessive/compulsive personalities. For them, work overtakes everything – their personal lives, relationships, even their health and well-being. Ultimately, they become less productive and rarely do they find real satisfaction from their work. They become distant from their families and other close relationships because they are oblivious to the art of negotiation and fail to understand that compromise is crucial for intimacy. They either marry someone who is subservient and easily controlled, or someone who is similarly controlling. In the latter case, the attraction is not only the spouse's strength of character, but their independent nature means they make few demands. If they allow their spouse to be the decision maker on the domestic front, the couple might get by, but if they attempt to relate to them as they do with business colleagues, disaster looms large.

These leaders apply their strict work ethic to their staff, not appreciating that they might not be able to run as fast or jump as high. They rely on adrenaline and enjoy their supply of it being fuelled by deadlines and crises at work to help them to continually operate at a manic pace. Work, for them, is the principal means of supporting their fragile self-esteem.

The workaholic's obsessive/compulsive nature is not uniform, and one trait can dominate the other. For example, while the obsessive person procrastinates, in contrast the more compulsive person is impulsive. Each responds in opposing ways to manage similar anxieties. Both approaches aim to avoid unpleasant feelings – one by overthinking, the other by overdoing. Obsessives are reluctant to make a move because they fear making a wrong decision and pine for an uncertainty-free outcome. They spend so much time examining all the pros and cons and assessing every worst-case scenario that no choice looks good and nothing gets done. The compulsive person, however, leaps into action to avoid uncomfortable thoughts and unpredictable results.

George Bernard Shaw, the renowned Irish playwright and wit, reportedly had a conversation with the great dancer Isadora Duncan along the following lines. She suggested that with his magnificent brain and her glorious beauty, they could produce a remarkable child. Shaw replied waspishly that he feared the resulting offspring might instead embody his beauty and her brains.

That anecdote came to mind in regard to Lucy, another of my clients. She had the good fortune to match Duncan's intended outcome by inheriting her father's acute intelligence and her mother's good looks. But that was not the end of the story. She also inherited her father's drive, perfectionism and workaholic nature together with her mother's sensitivity and deep anxiety.

Lucy is a warm, articulate and receptive person. Her exquisitely styled outfits and hair exemplify her perfectionistic nature and mask her insecurities. While her hesitant voice hints at self-doubt, you nevertheless quickly know you are in the company of an intelligent, serious person. The educational video business she had launched eight years previously was doing well but her lifelong workaholism and perfectionism were so ingrained that the thought of relaxing control filled her with dread. She might occasionally dip her toes in the waters of uncertainty but then was likely to panic and revert to compulsive behaviour in the hope of achieving the best results.

Lucy was not without self-awareness. This partly restrained her from imposing her excessively high standards on to staff. But when their work was not up to scratch, she corrected it herself. As a consequence, her employees never learnt for themselves or fully discovered what she expected from them, and she missed an opportunity to ascertain their capabilities.

'If you're always giving people a task and then taking it away in order to complete it to the higher standard, you don't become good at explaining how they should be doing it in future,' she said.

Her perfectionism meant she worked excessively but was unable to meet her expectations. Yet at the same time she dismissed her achievements. The effect was that she overworked and got sucked into details to the point where she would lose the bigger picture.

'I'm happy that people take things in their own direction but when it comes to my own work it's got to be 100 per cent perfect otherwise I feel out of control. It affects my self-esteem and I doubt myself if it's not perfect.'

Her work ethic informed her management style above all else, which made me ask her: 'What pushes your buttons most?'

'If I see someone kick back [taking it easy], that irritates me much more than people floundering or getting it wrong. I couldn't have someone in my team who was a real clock watcher.'

Lucy the perfectionist also procrastinates. Often the two go hand in hand. When she cannot see an obvious solution to a piece of work she panics and puts it off. 'My mind gets foggy and if I can't see that I can control the outcome, then I'm too afraid to even start on it.

'Overwork in its own way is a kind of procrastination,' she added. 'If I'm trying to compose the perfect email I might spend an hour writing it when another person would spend five minutes. I'll get to the end of the day and think, "What have I actually done?" And then you feel even worse because if you're a perfectionist you're also worried about how much you are achieving in a given day.'

'Being caught in a cycle of perfectionism and procrastination means much of your overworking is unnecessary,' I said. 'And you never feel satisfied.'

She concurred with this. 'I'll pick holes in whatever I've achieved. Even if it's an amazing outcome I'll always see an opportunity that was missed, like, we could have achieved it cheaper or quicker. If the outcome isn't what was planned, or the meeting doesn't go well, I go to "I'm a failure, I should have done that instead." Physically, I'll feel sick and full of self-doubt, like I've got to make amends and correct it – instead of chalking it up to experience.'

Lucy's driving motivation was to avoid the distress of criticism or the horror of a client disliking the result and sending the work back. Yet this in turn creates a dilemma.

'If you overwork' I said, 'you still feel bad because of the impact on your family [she has a husband and three children] and even if you do well, you dismiss your achievements. You're caught in a cycle of setting extraordinarily high expectations and when you can't meet them, you berate yourself and believe the only way to escape the cycle is to achieve more.'

She nodded in agreement, frustrated with the realisation. When we looked further back, it turned out her inheritance from her father was a double-edged sword. He was a classic control freak and workaholic. An ambitious barrister, he imposed the same strict standards he had for himself on to his only daughter. If she failed to meet his expectations, he would express disapproval.

'In my head I equate not achieving with being rejected or not being good enough to warrant attention. If I don't do a great job, I feel it's a slight on my personality. I really feel it's personal – not a work thing but a deep personal failing.

'I was repeatedly told I was not good enough,' she added. The goalposts would always be shifting. Every exam would be, "Now that you've accomplished that, next time you have to work more quickly or with less stress."'

Lucy had also suffered from cancer in her early teens, in addition to the emotional trauma of a bullying father and a weak mother who could not protect her from paternal excesses.

'With all the cancer and trauma, work was something I could control,' she explained. 'I was good at school and work. You put loads in and you get a good result – it's controllable. It's also rewarding. It's just that I don't know where the limits are.'

Overworking and perfectionism offered temporary relief from her anxiety. But even this had limits because when she was highly anxious she was unable to focus, which impinged on her performance.

She explained: 'When I have little work, I'm at my most anxious. It provides a distraction and intellectual engagement which I think helps me not to panic and stops my brain from spiralling.'

Having three young children had forced her to challenge some of her work habits. 'They've legitimately given me that break, or that necessity to switch off, but in other ways it's much harder because I feel I'm doing everything badly, which as a perfectionist is really horrible. I feel pulled, permanently.'

After we had worked together for some time, Lucy reflected on what had come out of our sessions that she had found particularly helpful: 'Building awareness about my behaviour has really helped. You once said, "Never is everything going to be ticked off the to-do list – you have to get used to the feeling of it being not done." What I'm trying to do more is live with that discomfort of things not being perfect in the hope that it will release me from the pressure it puts on my body and my family.'

Many become controlling and obsessively self-sufficient because they were unable to rely on parents or carers who were neglectful, abusive or chaotic. Being let down by colleagues at work can reignite the helplessness, fear and hostility they have repressed from childhood. The dependency they encounter in close working relationships is uncomfortable precisely because it feels like the first dependency they experienced in their family.

But though dependency is not comfortable for many people, it is necessary for collaboration and delegation. Dependency is sometimes frowned upon but all relationships, to a greater or lesser extent, require a degree of it. Believing that it is all up to you is neither realistic nor useful. Self-sufficiency might have been the wisest response to a chaotic family life, but does little to prepare one for relating and collaborating in the workplace. A company's success needs to be shared. Overestimating your role negates others' ideas, staff input, economic context and even the element that luck plays.

While it is good to trust colleagues and employees, trust does need to be cultivated by actual experience. It is not an absolute but an ongoing process. People are unpredictable – someone who has been trustworthy in a particular context or on a specific project may let you down in another and this makes controlling people particularly uncomfortable. Many leaders and business founders have complained to me that some of their worst errors of judgement were in placing trust in the wrong people. I often say to clients that the person they most need to trust is themselves – that they can read situations accurately, know what can reasonably be expected from staff and how to regain trust once it is lost.

If you have experienced a controlling boss, you will know how difficult it is to deal with them. Some can be challenged and others not. The best approach is to find out what they are worried about and convince them, by your words and actions, that you want to help. Often they need the same reassurance and security we all do. Ask yourself if what is expected of you is reasonable or not. Remember it is a two-way relationship. Try sentences such as this: 'In order for me to help you, I need to know such and such,' or, 'For me to do my job best, we need to work differently.' Once you have achieved a degree of trust, challenging them and receiving a positive outcome is more likely.

When dealing with bullies and tyrants, however, it is more a matter of survival and damage-limitation than resolution. If you find you have lost confidence and a sense of self at work to the extent you fear you have become unemployable, it is likely you have taken on their feelings of inadequacy and made them your own. In such circumstances, individuals mistakenly believe they need their boss's approval to regain their own confidence. Think about such a relationship as you would any abusive one – which it is. It can be difficult to untangle yourself if your self-belief has been eroded to the point where you believe the problem lies with you and not your bullying boss. If so, a coach or therapist is essential in identifying where reality lies. Once you are able to accept the failure is not yours but your boss's, you can build and bolster your determination to leave an unhealthy and unresolved situation. It is crucial to process this psychologically so that you do not take the bad feelings to your next job.

'It is always about relationships, and investing time in relationships really pays off,' says Professor Heffernan. 'A great deal of what people want from work is about freedom, and the freedom to explore and grow and be themselves. And to the degree to which you give them a good context to do that they will amaze you, and to the degree you control them they're always going to disappoint you – because really you want them to be you, not them.'

If you are a manager struggling to release control, you will need to accept that others will be able to do the job as well as you, and sometimes better. Let being liked be the last thing on your mind – it will only limit you in making good decisions. Know that mistakes and failures are inevitable. Try to see the opportunities in all outcomes. Either you will be successful, in which case you will need to pass on the credit to your team, or there will be something to learn from the failures.

Greg Hodder is a veteran executive of large companies whose experience has taught him many of these lessons. His career has included being chief executive of Charles Tyrwhitt, the menswear retailer, and Direct Wines, and chairman of Majestic Wines. He believes he made his greatest leap in management when making the shift from achieving satisfaction from his successes to gaining it from others doing well.

Leadership came naturally for him, although delegating responsibility and sharing success did not. Circumstances in early childhood forced him to be a leader in his own family after his father left when he was two years old. For as long as he could remember, he felt responsible for the family, especially his mother. The middle of three siblings, he recalls his mother treating him more like an adult than a child, never challenging him and leaving him to his own devices. Greg was never told what to do and this led to frequent clashes with authority at school. Soon he realised he was never going to be able to work for anyone. For him, the joy of business was being captain of the ship.

But during his impressive career, he nevertheless had to learn the art of delegating. Initially, he fell back on his instinct to control but soon realised this would limit the business. He believes that what he does best today is bring people in who are going to drive the business forward.

'Now, when I'm asked to do something, my first thought is, what needs to happen and then deciding the person who is going to do it,' he said. 'What has given me the most satisfaction is adding three or four very senior people and radically changing the business. And watching them hiring their own teams and having complete trust in them and them having complete trust in me.

'There is that moment that you realise the person who you're delegating to has just got it, and is performing the role better than you could ever have done, and is communicating well with you – that's one of the most fulfilling moments you can have in a management capacity.'

9

# Perils of the pedestal – why idealisation inevitably leads to a crash

My father loved to be loved. Fortunately, it was not difficult to love Fred. He was warm, cuddly and funny. There was no mistaking his need for love. Just one example: following repeated cardiac surgeries in middle age, doctors warned him there was nothing more they could do and he would have to change his lifestyle radically. They suggested he enter a cardiac rehabilitation programme that included group therapy. He emerged a different man, and began by replacing his business suits with jeans and an 'I Love to Hug' T-shirt and car bumper sticker to match.

His life until then had featured extreme drama, horror, migration, not to mention financial highs and lows. Fred was born into a Jewish middle class family that owned a department store in Miskolc, Hungary. During the Second World War, his family were rounded up by the Nazis and sent to Auschwitz where his parents were murdered as part of Hitler's 'Final Solution.' After the concentration camps were liberated in 1945, he joined the exodus of Holocaust survivors to Palestine and its growing Jewish homeland. In what subsequently became Israel, he met and married my mother, Alice, another Auschwitz survivor, and this was where my sister Ruth and I were born. When he found it increasingly difficult to support us there, we moved to America, with only $50 in our pockets and no English. Initially, Fred worked as a lorry driver while studying at night to be an accountant, but eventually became a licensed realtor in Los Angeles, bought a house, installed a swimming pool and joined the ranks of middle-class Jewish life.

Although he never had much interest in or patience for children, I never doubted that he loved me, as evidenced by the annual birthday rhymes he composed. There were also advantages, I found, to having an immigrant father. Everything I asked for, as long as I could convince him that it was normal in the US, I got. 'Everybody in America has a pony,' I insisted. Unable to bear the thought of not belonging or fitting in, he bought me a pony.

My mother, however, could not recognise the love Fred offered nor give him the love he craved – and so he turned his sights to business. His property-dealing aspirations were ambitious, but often failed. An exception was a mobile home park in Victorville, California, where he named streets after our family – there was Ruth Street, Alice Avenue, Fred Street and Naomi Avenue – our proud and heartwarming signs on the road to Las Vegas.

Many of his bad decisions resulted from a need to be admired, which was really a longing for love. The reasons for this stacked up: his father had bullied him as a child, the shattering grief of losing his parents, the horror of Auschwitz and then a loveless marriage. Whatever the origins, his craving was irresistible. In business, he often recruited young men who would look up to him approvingly – something his father and wife did not do. Often these inexperienced men were not nearly worth the money he paid, but they admired him.

Then, during the mid-1970s when I was in my teens, he returned to Hungary to show people there what a big-shot American he had become, which infuriated and confused me. How could a Holocaust survivor return to a country that had colluded in the deportation and murder of his family? How could he socialise with people who may have lined the streets and cheered as he and his family were taken away? Such was his need to be thought of highly.

Around this time, he suffered the heart attack that required quadruple bypass surgery and received that final warning from doctors – change your lifestyle or die. So he quit smoking and began exercising, walking around our swimming pool 120 times daily, using a counter to keep track. After resuming work, he involved himself with a group of young, sexy Swiss bankers who knew too well how to manipulate a middle-aged man who wanted to be accepted and admired. They persuaded him to mortgage the family home and invest the money in a property deal, but the fortune they promised never materialised. The money was lost and with it the family home, swimming pool and all. Once again my parents had lost everything – first to the Nazis and then to Swiss bankers. It also triggered the end of their marriage, and a breach in my relationship with my father.

After my parents' divorce, he lived in a small beach-front apartment in southern California. Someone mentioned that with his round belly, bushy white beard and hair, laughing eyes and broad smile, he resembled Santa Claus. That was all the encouragement he needed. He equipped himself with a

Santa suit – and not just a version for winter, which really does not exist in that part of California, but a summer one too, including shorts and surf board to match. Fully outfitted for the part, he embarked on work for charitable causes, particularly for sick, homeless or abused children, and relished the attention and adoration bestowed on him as a result. He became a local hero who featured in many a media article about this charming man. In such interviews he often fabricated stories about his life, for instance omitting the years we lived in Israel, his divorce from my mother – to my fury, he described himself as a widower – and even his family's Holocaust history. Any reference to his Jewishness might have blighted his Santa identity and with it the attention and adoration.

In my mid-twenties, I left for Europe and eventually made London my home. The distance helped to heal our relationship. I remembered his silly poems and big warmth. He visited me in London and our relationship flourished for the first time in years. But not long after he returned to California the dreaded phone call came. Fred had suffered another heart attack and died.

I believe that in his Santa Claus guise he finally felt loved. Was his quest so wrong? Yes, he made some terrible business decisions on the way, but in the end the lashings of adoration and appreciation healed something in him. The compassion he felt towards children was genuine and as Father Christmas he was able to open his heart and bring them moments of deep joy.

'I have a secret,' he once admitted to me. 'Everyone thinks I am so generous, but the truth is I do it for me.'

Fred is far from alone. We all seek love and validation. It helps cushion our fragile self-esteem against life's blows and boost the confidence we need to delve into the unknown and pursue our dreams. But for individuals who have an overwhelming compulsion to be thought of highly, esteem from others means more. As with my father, it might be an attempt to compensate for a difficult relationship with parents or to distance oneself from early bullying, loneliness or deep feelings of shame. In this regard work can often be a corrective, but sadly it often misses the mark because it is too superficial to profoundly improve self-regard. Instead, it leaves one only wanting more.

Leaders are not immune from this temptation because respect and admiration help maximise the self-belief required to manage large teams of people. A normal amount of healthy narcissism is not only useful but also necessary to climb to high positions and persuade others to follow you. But an excessive need for acclaim can also be one side of a two-sided coin – where a person's need for adoration matches the need of others to see their leader, or idol, as perfect. This is a mutual relationship with distortion on both sides. Heaping admiration on those in power sustains the fantasy that people we rely on are all-knowing and all good. Being close to people we believe are great also makes us feel better about ourselves, as if their brilliance rubs off on us. It is not only powerful people on who we bestow this privileged position, we can also idealise organisations, institutions and ideologies. When one is put on a pedestal and seen to do no wrong, however, both leaders and the organisations they run should worry.

The usual admiration we bestow on our leaders is no bad thing. People in such positions have immense responsibilities and challenges and they deserve respect and support. The danger is that admiration can give way to excessive reverence because of our unreasonable need to see people more powerful than us as perfect. In psychotherapy the need to see leaders as better than they are is known as 'idealisation.' We idealise people who have power over us because it makes us feel good – thinking our leaders can do no wrong makes us feel fortunate, safe, optimistic and eliminates potential doubts and disappointments.

As children, it is useful to believe our parents are perfect and omniscient because it sustains us against a harsh and unpredictable world. When we are small and overwhelmed with fears and feelings of helplessness, it is comforting to imagine the people who care for us know everything. But as we grow, reality dawns and we need to acknowledge that our parents are not superhuman but flawed. In time, we learn to rely more on our own minds and accept that the world is an imperfect place. Yet it is tempting as adults not to shed the misapprehension of childhood entirely and believe that others we depend on, particularly those with authority over us, can fulfil our fantasies of complete security and protection when feelings of hopelessness arise. In this comforting fantasy, however, danger lies.

Manfred Kets de Vries expressed to me the danger inherent in idealisation in the workplace: 'It's a totally reinforcing dance in which – because of a general feeling of helplessness – you idealise the leader and say quickly what the leader likes, what the leader wants to hear, and that reinforces the leader's narcissism and vice versa. Unfortunately, the moment the leader accepts this, he is surrounded by liars. There are people who always give positive feedback – everything is so perfect. You start to believe you have an echo chamber.'

Idealisation offers a reassuring distraction from the harsh realities of working life. But it blurs the limits of leaders' capabilities and exaggerates how genuinely interested they are in their staff and the security they provide. When adoring employees insist on protecting their boss, they revert to locating any faults elsewhere – in a competing company, a disgruntled team or even themselves. Attempting to gain the leader's approval, followers are likely to say what he or she wants to hear and suppress their own good ideas. More dangerously, they can brush aside or excuse their boss's misconduct. In this way, idealisation can allow a leader to act irresponsibly or unethically. For leaders, it is tempting to believe in the adoration bestowed on them and even in their own mythology, oblivious to their faults.

When a leader's flaws are exposed, which is inevitable because we are all imperfect, the fall from grace can be monumental. The magnitude almost certainly depends on the degree of distortion. The higher one is put on a pedestal, the greater the fall. And perhaps one of the saddest outcomes is that any good work a leader has accomplished is quickly forgotten.

That was the case for Kids Company, a leading UK charity for disadvantaged children that collapsed in 2015 amid allegations of gross financial mismanagement. Its founder and chief executive was the remarkable Camila Batmanghelidjh. Everything about her oozed charisma, from her persuasive charm and gregarious personality to her flamboyant dress style of primary coloured robes and turbans. All this, combined with her work for underprivileged children, helped elevate her to celebrity status and such renown that for nearly two decades the charity's administration was unchallenged by public watchdogs such as the media, politicians, charity and other authorities.

From the time of Kids Company's launch in 1996 to its collapse, it was allocated over £42 million in government grants and received hundreds of millions of pounds from the public and philanthropists. Donors included business executives and rock stars, such as Richard Branson and Coldplay, and support came from prime ministers Gordon Brown and David Cameron. Batmanghelidjh's rise to celebrity status was further aided by the fact that supporting righteous causes makes people feel wonderful about themselves.

When the charity's financial problems became apparent – compounded by allegations of sexual abuse against it that police later found to be groundless – her fall from grace was total. Rather than being given the benefit of the doubt, much of the good work her charity had achieved was forgotten as two House of Commons reports condemned the charity's management and lack of scrutiny by the government. In 2015, the public accounts committee said tens of millions of government grants were spent by the charity without proper assessment of whether it achieved value for money. A year later, the Commons public administration and constitutional affairs committee pinned the charity's failure on a combination of 'negligent' trustees and the 'unaccountable and dominant' Batmanghelidjh. In 2021, however, the High Court cleared Batmanghelidjh and the charity's trustees of claims by the Official Receiver that they had failed to properly manage the charity – but by then the damage to her status had been done. Many children benefited from her and the charity's work but ultimately it would be remembered wrongly for a financial 'scandal'.

The danger of idealisation increases when leaders appear to begin to believe their own myths and ignore allegations of misconduct. Such was the case for Elizabeth Holmes, founder and CEO of Theranos, a California-based blood-testing start-up, who, it is alleged, continued to promote her company's so-called achievements even when faced with allegations of fraudulent behaviour.

Holmes was only 19 years old in 2003 when she quit Stanford University to start the company; she subsequently became the youngest self-made female billionaire. At one point, her company was valued at $9 billion. Theranos claimed to be able to detect many illnesses from a single drop of blood through its tiny 'nanotainer' devices and analytic machines. She vowed to revolutionise medicine and change the world through cheap and efficient blood tests that could offer early diagnosis of numerous illnesses. The *Wall Street Journal*, however, alleged that the machines were defective and many blood samples were not tested in Theranos laboratories but sent to other companies to be analysed. More seriously, it claimed that her company had put patient safety at risk as a result of impaired blood tests. It also alleged that not only had she lied to investors, she had also threatened any staff who complained that Theranos's tests were not working.

By 2018, Holmes was facing several federal fraud charges as well as civil suits. She denies the fraud charges. Her federal trial, delayed by the coronavirus pandemic, is due in 2021.

Holmes captured the imagination of not only the public but more importantly investors, her board of directors and the press. An attractive and ultra-confident young entrepreneur, she modelled herself on her idol Steve Jobs, wearing the same black turtlenecks and even lowering her voice to sound more masculine. Her hypnotic stare seemed to mesmerise people. Even hard-bitten journalists were swayed by her aura. She appeared in photo shoots alongside such figures as former US presidents Bill Clinton and Barack Obama. Investors believed that she could radically disrupt and change medicine. Her board attracted some of the best and experienced minds of its generation, including former US Secretaries of State Henry Kissinger and George Schultz, and James Mattis, who went on to be Secretary of Defence. Could the board members have been so entranced that they believed she was a genius and allegedly ignored warning signs? Schultz is said to have even ignored evidence of malpractice presented to him by his grandson, who worked in Theranos's laboratories.

Could investors, who pumped $700 million into the company, her board and politicians have become so besotted by her promises of transforming medicine that they ignored information in exchange for a marvellous story? Why would intelligent people, and hugely experienced investors, put their reputations at risk?

Facts, it turns out, are not just facts, they also create feeling. Bad news and complexity make us anxious, while certainty, as told through an optimistic story, relieves our anxiety. Clarity and simple explanations are more likely to be accepted because they make us feel better and spare us uncomfortable information. We wish it to be true.

Reducing people to either all knowing or all bad is similar to the psychological defence of splitting as described in chapter one. Our desire to create black-and-white explanations avoids the complexities of personalities, businesses and organisations, and their strengths and weaknesses. Our wish that people and organisations can solve complex problems is enticing but risky. Of course leaders and their ideas require some faith on our part to succeed but this needs to be balanced by realistic regard for their limitations.

Hero worshipping leaders, whether celebrity ones or heads of mundane companies, rid us of ambivalence and ensure that any negative emotions we may be harbouring – such as anger, hostility, even hatred – never enter the idealised relationship. Close working relationships are bound to elicit bad feelings from time to time. Yet when these feelings are denied in order to keep the boss on a pedestal, they can become internalised – so the individual ends up feeling bad about themselves – or displaced on to other relationships. Often such thoughts are not denied completely but pushed to the back of one's mind so as not to disturb the comfort of a perfect union. We may, for example, hold a sneaking suspicion that our organisation is not so perfect but we dare not allow such worrying thoughts to enter the forefront of our mind where it can disrupt our optimism and enthusiasm.

It requires emotional maturity and mental effort to tolerate conflicting feelings about a person, to recognise their talents and weaknesses, virtues and vices. And for individuals lacking this ability, when they finally do recognise the flaws in the idealised person, they might well disregard all the good attributes they have previously so admired. It is too easy to see the other as all good or all bad. Furthermore, recognising a leader's limitations may involve taking more responsibility oneself, perhaps even taking action where misconduct exists and losing the leader's favour. Acknowledging that your boss has always supported you but treated others unfairly is a difficult pill to swallow and may leave you feeling guilty. Or that your manager promoted you but then takes all the credit for your excellent work. It is being able to tolerate such contradictions that helps to see a person as they truly are and prepares you best to do your job.

A distinction can be made between idealisation and glorification. Glorification involves politicians and celebrities, people who are far removed from our lives. Idealisation usually occurs with people close to us – and even those who have less power than we do. One can idealise co-workers, managers can idealise employees and individuals their organisations and missions. This dynamic is often what underpins favouritism when the boss is enthralled by someone they perceive as exceptionally talented or a rising star. Whereas glorification is conscious, idealisation is often unconscious and therefore more difficult to spot and deal with.

As a leader, if you find that everyone is agreeing with you

and not giving any bad feedback, you should question it. It might mean that you have encouraged, knowingly or not, an idealised view of yourself to an extent that concerns and problems remain unstated because staff fear bursting your bubble. To counteract this, you should positively seek negative feedback and dissenting ideas. It is also crucial to show some vulnerability and expose your humanity. Asking questions tells your team that you do not know it all. The saying 'it's lonely at the top' is too true. The higher one is elevated, the more one can be remote and isolated. Making yourself visible and spending time with employees will diminish the distance that can fuel their perfectionistic fantasies. The discomfort of revealing your vulnerabilities will, in the long run, prevent a painful future fall when, inevitably, you slip off the pedestal. Managers should take heed – it is far easier to prevent idealisation than to deal with the aftermath of its crash.

It should be said that there is a useful and creative aspect of idealisation. Staff can feel inspired and energised, and generally better about themselves, when they idealise their boss or the organisation they work for. But yet again, this has dangers, as Manfred Kets de Vries describes in his book, *The Leader on the Couch*. 'Many executives create idealistic, powerful images of the organisations in which they work,' he writes. This 'fantasy' of the organisation or company can be profoundly cherished by employees to the extent that they 'feel stronger, more adequate and more capable.' This encourages them to strive for the ideal image they have in their minds. Yet such extreme identification with their employer and its leader impairs their personal judgement, leading to an idealisation that 'suggests the organisation is incapable of error.' This in turn will prevent change and make failure more likely as the company collectively ceases learning from experience. 'After all, there's no need to learn from mistakes when mistakes are impossible,' he concludes.

Such a fantasy of perfection, the belief that 'we can do anything together,' is precisely what drove Robert and his partner Sam to heights of success at first but eventually led to financial loss and the end of their relationship. Robert is an entrepreneur in his late thirties who began a media start-up venture with his business partner, Sam, who is 12 years his junior.

Robert is friendly, extremely polite and always arrived to our meetings casually dressed and bang on time. He made a long journey from Bristol to London and appreciated the cup of tea I offered when he entered the front door. With a to-do list in hand, he was invariably eager to begin and tackle issues in the 90 minutes we set aside.

He first sought my advice when tensions between the partners had escalated to an extent they were unable to either deal with problems or take the business forward. It felt particularly personal because not only did they have a ten-year business relationship but also a close friendship. This all left Robert depressed and doubting himself. Although generally successful in his career and happily married, he was confused and feeling hopeless. Our work helped to untangle a business partnership that was causing professional damage and personal heartache.

Robert told me that he and Sam met at work, a friendship developed and eventually they became business partners. I asked him about their early relationship. 'Initially, I felt it was one of the best friendships I had ever had,' he said. 'I [had never] experienced such respect and admiration from someone who I respected. That was the first time I experienced someone looking up to me where it mattered. I wasn't used to someone saying how great I was – nobody I gave a toss about. In those early years, I could do no wrong. It felt really good and made me feel close to him.'

Arguments in their early days were few and far between, as Robert explained. 'If we disagreed it would get a little bit heated but then he would back down. He would then tend to see my point of view and there was a sense of regret from him in the following days. We just seemed to get stronger from those things.'

They entered their industry at a fruitful time and their company soon became something of a powerhouse. It seemed to flourish magically. Although Robert had good business sense, there was an element of timing and luck involved. Their financial success gave them a false sense of security and belief that they 'could conquer the world.'

Although Sam had thought more highly of Robert than vice versa, their dynamic became one of mutual pumping up of the other's self-belief. But their deluded sense of what they could actually achieve led to some disastrous business decisions. The lengthy honeymoon ended because each had branched out to expand the business in different directions, acted hastily and made some bad moves. Robert impulsively entrusted one of their businesses to two shady characters who were subsequently responsible for the loss of nearly £1.5 million.

Robert reflected: 'We started to embark on some new projects that turned out to be absolute disasters. We didn't have our eye on the ball. He would pretty much back me on anything I wanted to do and consequently I would back him on anything he wanted to do. We supported each other to such a degree that if one believed it was a good thing to do then it would get the full backing of the other. If he and I believed it as the CEOs, then everyone else went along with it. We had too much belief in ourselves and too much belief in each other.

'The largest factor was that we were doing so well [financially]. When people around you are saying you're doing so well it can go to your head. You can end up in a delusional state. It wasn't down to lack of wisdom or experience – it was down to being caught up in the moment and getting an overinflated sense of what you can achieve.'

While the financial loss was devastating, what played most on Robert's mind was losing Sam's admiration. 'I remember having to call Sam and say to him, "This has gone wrong – this is potentially how much we're going to lose." The confrontation wasn't difficult; I was agonising over the fact that he'd be disappointed in me. I said: "I hope you haven't lost faith in me." He didn't completely and utterly reassure me that he hadn't lost faith in me – I think he did.'

After that they gradually became more distant and had more disputes and Sam began to disagree on nearly every point. His belief that Robert was 100 per cent trustworthy had evaporated and he lost all faith in him. Robert's fall was to be irretrievable, and their partnership never recovered. Sam's disappointment unleashed a torrent of negative feelings and Sam now saw Robert as a figure of contempt and disdain.

In order to understand Robert's vulnerability to idealisation, we examined his family's story. He was the middle of three sons of a father who suffered from schizophrenia. Of the three, Robert was tasked with taking responsibility for their mother's well-being. If she were to succumb to the stress of looking after her husband, there would be nobody to look after him and his brothers. This gave him a tremendous sense of responsibility, which began his early training as a business leader. There was more, too. His father was too ill to provide the encouragement and praise he craved. And in addition, he suffered deep feelings of shame and humiliation because he and his family were mocked by other children and neighbours because of his father's illness.

'I had low self-esteem coming into my teens and that was quite largely due to growing up with my dad's illness and then experiences in school. I don't think I had enough adulation from the right sort of people – mainly from my mum.'

Determined not to identify with a father whose working life had been cut short by mental illness, he was driven to achieve and not replicate his father's failure in this regard. His life, he decided, would be nothing like his father's. Having taken responsibility for his family, he knew instinctively how to run a business and care for his staff. As a result, he developed a strong and loyal team who were committed to the company because he invested in them. More importantly, it was crucial for him to be seen as 'normal' and not 'ill.' Anything that could be construed as 'abnormal,' or like his father, would make him panic. Success would also shield him from the mockery he and his family experienced. The admiration gushing from Sam bolstered this but when it abruptly came to a halt, Robert's fears of being humiliated and unloved were reignited.

'Sam offered something you lacked – a man who believed in you and thought you were remarkable,' I suggested. 'With Sam, you sought what your father could not provide.'

'Definitely,' he responded. 'Even the close friendships I had in school, I was always the inferior one, never the frontrunner. And then at home, my dad – I always knew he loved me but he wasn't the sort of person to build up your self-esteem or that you could look up to, sadly.'

After the financial loss, Robert put much personal and professional work over many months into meticulously dividing up the business, which ultimately meant the partnership with Sam ended amicably and Robert was able to retain the beneficial aspects of their relationship. Furthermore, he now has more belief in himself and emerged more optimistic. He went on to achieve success on his own, which has undoubtedly played a part in his transformation.

'I've gone from being a meek and weak child to quite a powerful personality – not a domineering personality, but my self-awareness means I know that I have an effect on people and I try to use that in a positive way. Things have changed.'

For every leader such as Robert who craves to be idealised, there are followers with an equivalent need to see their leaders as exceptional. In Robert's case, Sam would have had his own reasons for looking up to Robert with such absolute faith. His dependent nature meant he sought security and safety from his partner, with the outcome that rather than realising that Robert was as prone to mistakes as the best of us, he put him on a pedestal. When he inevitably fell, he fell hard. As Robert described it: 'I went from being a ten out of ten to a five out of ten. I'd really fallen from grace.'

It is often those with dependent and insecure personalities who need to feed off the strength of their leaders – or at least, the imagined strength. They frequently struggle to make decisions, have little faith in themselves and need to believe that someone with a better mind can decide for them and provide security.

Authority figures at work can trigger longings for the safety that was inadequate in one's early life. In that case, there may exist two authority figures in someone's mind: the actual one who has disappointed and an idealised one who offers perfect protection. For such individuals, the longing for a 'perfect parent' can be strong. Being looked on favourably by their boss can ignite this need and propel the person to behave in a way that elicits the desired reaction.

This was the case for a middle-aged woman, Elise, who worked for a charity. After a period in therapy, the realisation of who her boss actually was, as opposed to the idealised version she had created in her mind, led her to examine not only her own professional life but also her early years and relationship with her mother.

She said of her boss: 'I had her on a pedestal, I thought she was great, super-intelligent, top of her game in her field and I was lucky to be alongside her.'

In her mind, her manager represented the ideal mother – someone who believed that she, Elise, was accomplished and treated her as such. Early in their professional relationship, her boss even offered emotional support and advice on dealing with boyfriends. Although her boss was unfair and at times bullying towards other employees, Elise felt more than protected, she felt special. Confusing her boss's appreciation for genuine care touched a deep need in her for security and love. Eliciting her boss's admiration, however, was contingent on making herself available to her every demand, even to the detriment of her family.

Elise explained how she was manipulated: 'She had me believe [that] I'm amazingly intelligent. I had to work so hard to be the golden girl. I used to let her call me anytime day or night, weekends or evenings. I would drop everything as if nothing to do with me could be as important. I would panic at not answering the phone when she rang. I even made a separate ringtone so that I would know if she was calling – even at the expense of ruining my children's bedtime routine because I would leave them in front of the television when she needed me.'

Once she gained these realisations in therapy, her behaviour towards her boss changed. She began to voice her opinions and ceased her more extreme pleasing behaviour. The halo effect dissolved quickly and her boss reacted aggressively when Elise made herself less available, further escalating tensions between them. Their unspoken agreement had been breached by Elise's new-found assertiveness, and her privileged position, which had been contingent on idealising her boss, ended. Ultimately, it cost Elise her job – she was made redundant.

'Looking at her now, without the rose-coloured specs on, I see I was living a lie. The end was a disaster because I started to have strong opinions and to see that she wasn't as great as I thought she was.'

Looking back to her early years, Elise described a mother who was emotionally neglectful and physically absent. She divorced her husband and became a single mother when Elise was only a year old. Elise remembers her frequently giving boyfriends precedence over her three young children, leaving them with babysitters when she had a better offer.

'When we were at home she was very aggressive because it was very stressful being a single mother. I didn't ever feel that she looked after me, I never felt safe. She would often go to bed before me and my siblings. So I would lock the front door at night. She wouldn't tuck us in and make sure we were OK.'

Although she could allow herself these recollections when sitting in my consulting room many years later, as a child, she could not bear to think of her mother as harming her and instead idealised her beauty, intelligence and lifestyle. Seeing her mother for who she actually was – someone who neglected her children in pursuit of her own pleasure – would have been too terrifying a prospect for a young child to face. Instead, she defended against such disturbing thoughts by, paradoxically, thinking of her as perfect.

In reality, attention from her mother was fleeting at best. As a child, she learnt to tune into her mother's every need to sustain what little attention was offered. Attending to others' needs while neglecting her own was therefore how Elise learnt to connect with others and ensure she would not be forgotten or left entirely alone. Years later, she repeated the same pattern with her boss. 'I knew how to be what she wanted me to be, to keep her interested in me,' she said. While the cost of idealisation was high it was also familiar – it was what she knew.

As I mentioned earlier, idealisation is a mutual dance between one who demands admiration and another's need to admire. In Elise's case, putting her boss on a pedestal defended her against feelings of helplessness stemming from her childhood. It also perpetuated the gap between the fantasy (her imagined boss) and the reality (her actual boss). And finally, it protected her from having to face the harm her mother caused. When her boss fell from grace, so did her mother.

However, this dance could not occur without the agreement of both. While I focused on Elise's need to admire, her boss's excessive demand for admiration and her extremely exploitative behaviour are more indicative of narcissistic personality disorder. But more of that in the next chapter.

The saying, 'if it looks too good to be true, it probably is too good to be true,' can apply equally to people. If you find yourself believing you have the perfect boss or are star-struck with your new employee, you might be in the grip of idealisation.

Here are points to help determine whether you are struggling with idealisation rather than normal admiration:

- You believe your boss has all the answers.
- You find yourself agreeing with him or her to the extent you hold back good ideas.

- Pleasing your boss overrides attending to your professional development.
- Your need for your chief's approval exceeds your need for this in personal relationships.
- You've lost confidence and believe you can regain it only through your boss's validation.

It is much easier to prevent idealisation than repair the damage. The following will help leaders guard against it:

- Showing vulnerability can counter the tendency to be seen as omniscient.
- If you are not hearing negative feedback you should actively seek it out.
- Asking for help occasionally demonstrates that you do not have all the answers.
- Convince your staff that you welcome disagreement and differing views.
- Make yourself visible and available to staff.

10

# In defence of (most) narcissists – and what we get wrong about them

Thanks to one man, the subject of narcissism has gained a much wider currency since 2016. Step forward the forty-fifth president of the United States, Donald J. Trump. He put the subject on the map because his behaviour and character tick just about every box for those with a narcissistic personality disorder, otherwise referred to as malignant or pathological narcissism.

Narcissism is not always pathological, but rather a personality trait of widely varying degrees. Those at its more destructive extreme have an insatiable appetite for control, status and praise. They are often compelling and charismatic characters who can draw people under their spell – until difficulties and conflict arise and their deeper, darker personality emerges. Witness the self-obsessed chief with a volatile temper who both charms and intimidates staff, and takes all the credit for success while shifting blame for failures on to his underlings.

While many mental health experts believe Trump to be an extreme narcissist, there is little recognition that behind his larger-than-life facade resides a fearful self who feels small and victimised. In a 2020 article for *Medium*, the online publishing platform, psychoanalyst Michael Bader took a deep look into the workings of Trump's mind to examine how guilt and shame have haunted him since he was made to feel helpless as a child by a bullying father.

Dr Bader explains:

> When someone is rendered helpless at any stage in life, that person becomes prone to self-blaming – namely, guilt – and to feel shame. But, because our minds continually seek to avoid and eliminate distressing internal states, such a person is desperately motivated to get rid of these feelings at all costs.
>
> And so what does he do? He makes sure that they never make an appearance in his [Trump's] psyche. If they threaten to show up, they have to be somehow mitigated or banished immediately. He uses denial to ignore reality ("I won the popular vote in 2016 if you deduct the millions of people who voted illegally"). He is constantly projecting, positioning himself as the one being hurt rather than the one hurting others ("The Democrats' impeachment inquiry is a lynching"). And he stamps out any vestige of shame by sanitising and fashioning a self that is "perfect" – a self that is sparkling clean, beautiful, all-knowing and all-powerful.

Dr Bader continues by pointing out that Trump cannot regard defeats as political, only as highly personal. (Once again, in 2020 he falsely claimed that his presidential election defeat was because of electoral fraud.) Any semblance of failure envelops him in shame and anger. 'For Trump, losing equals loser equals shame ... His dread of being a small, flawed, helpless loser is so powerful that he has had to fashion a self that is the absolute opposite,' he adds. 'The truth – reality – can never stand in the way of these efforts.'

So, thanks largely to Trump, it is little wonder that narcissists get such a bad press these days. Trump is not the only leading figure to be described as such, of course. Tycoons such as Apple's Steve Jobs have been similarly branded, alongside their extraordinary achievements. Indeed, while such figures have brought narcissism to public attention, they may have also misled people into believing that most leaders and chief executives suffer from the disorder. In fact, narcissist chief executives are not nearly as prevalent as one might expect. Evidence for this view was supported by a 2016 study carried out by Professor Patrick Wright and colleagues at the Centre for Executive Succession, Darla Moore School of Business, at the University of South Carolina. They found that only 5 per cent of CEOs surveyed could clearly be classified as narcissists, whereas 60 per cent were described as scoring high in humility. So, in other words, CEOs were 12 times more likely to be humble than narcissistic. The results suggest that you have only a one in 20 chance of working for a narcissistic chief. That is not to suggest that such leaders cannot cause an inordinate amount of damage to companies and the individuals who work for them, only to keep a perspective on the prevalence of extreme narcissists.

Since Trump's rise to global attention, the term tends to be thrown about recklessly whenever anyone behaves badly, selfishly or even exhibits considerable drive and ambition. As a result, there has been no shortage of advice in the media as how to recognise, survive or recover from a narcissist. Organisational psychologists have researched the damage to companies (or not) when led by such an individual. And we are intrigued and baffled by these individuals.

Yet 'narcissism' is one of the most misunderstood and overused terms among personality types. The first misconception is that it is a condition someone has 'caught', like a contagious disease. No one is born with it either, although its roots can be located as early as infancy. We also tend to condemn narcissism in others while failing to recognise it in ourselves. The writer Gore Vidal put it succinctly when he defined a narcissist as, 'someone who is better looking than you are.'

In fact, we are all, to a greater or lesser degree, narcissistic. Without a certain amount of narcissism we would not muster the confidence needed to apply for a challenging job, have the guts to promote a new idea or even assert authority when it is rightfully ours. In other words, a healthy dose of it is not just beneficial but crucial to get ahead in our careers. Healthy narcissism is the belief we have in ourselves, it fuels our ambitions and provides the toughness we need at times to persevere. We need it to assert our opinions, challenge others and take professional risks and innovate.

At the low extreme of the narcissism spectrum are those individuals who have a deficiency of it. They lack self-belief, avoid risk and are inept at assertion skills. Disagreements are a terrifying prospect because they cannot stand up for themselves. They tend to be led by others rather than making their own way and, while this might make them good team players, they are not game changers or innovators.

Further along are those who have a healthy self-regard

or healthy narcissism. Their confidence and optimism are grounded in reality while coupled with empathy and a willingness to admit mistakes. While they have ambition and drive, they are not so ruthless as to torment others in pursuit of their aspirations, as we see in those at the more extreme end. They can ask for help and enjoy others' successes. They take pride in their work and pleasure in their accomplishments. These are not just healthy traits but essential for successful leaders. These people are sometimes referred to as productive narcissists because they get things done. What sets them apart from malignant narcissists is their capacity for self-reflection and ability to consider others' needs and feelings. Although they may well be sensitive to criticism, they can accept challenging feedback if they see it is in their interest, and the company's, to do so.

At the furthest extreme of the spectrum is the malignant narcissist. Their real hallmark is a lack of empathy and sense of entitlement. While they share the ambition and vision of healthy narcissists, arrogance about their own capabilities knows no bounds and in pursuit of goals they take no prisoners. They care greatly about what others think of them but have little time for or interest in others unless it is to their own advantage. Extreme narcissists have an insatiable appetite for admiration and this is why they go to great lengths to sound and look great, and even display some compassion from time to time if they believe it will burnish their credentials as a leader. But hidden behind the self-assured allure is a very thin skin and deep fragility.

Distrust is a prominent characteristic. Malignant narcissists are constantly looking out for enemies and perceive slights, criticisms and differing views as threats to their self-esteem. When experiencing shame or humiliation, rather than recognising that such unwanted emotions reside internally, they wrongly conclude others have intended to offend them and respond with outbreaks of rage. This can lead to paranoia, an 'either you're with me or against me' mentality. They see life as a zero-sum game and people as either winners or losers. Naturally, they surround themselves with perceived winners while discarding losers. As Dr Bader points out in his analysis of Trump's mind, feeling a loser risks triggering emotions they find intolerable. To reassure their perception of themselves as winners, they make others feel like losers by either discarding them or projecting their own 'loser' traits on to them.

Some seduce their subordinates into feeling important and exceptional. Indeed, this explains why individuals with low self-worth find themselves drawn to these leaders. Yet while this can be a strength it is also a trap. The fleeting praise can be so satisfying as to motivate one to strive and achieve more but this can also be a journey down an ever more complex rabbit hole that ultimately results in acclaim for them but little for you. The sooner you can accept the harsh truth that all garlands of praise will be hung around their necks, rather than yours, the better.

One managing director at a New York company never knew what to expect from his narcissistic chief. 'I had no idea whether he'd praise me to the skies or damn me as the most useless individual that ever lived,' he explained. 'The inconsistencies and the unpredictability is one of the things that makes working for a person like this so stressful. If they were uniformly hostile and horrible you'd know that was what you were dealing with.

'He was in one of two modes with me: I was either doing a brilliant job and he proved his own judgement in promoting me – it was always a positive reflection on him. Mode two was furious anger at me for things I'd done wrong. He had a terrible temper and that temper went along with quite infantile behaviour, like throwing whatever came to hand down on his desk.'

Yet the managing director recognised the CEO's exceptional talents, such as fierce intelligence and capacity for arduous work. 'There was a positive side to his narcissism – he was also extremely productive and efficient and good at getting things done. At the end, I had to say he was very good at his job. It would pain me to say it, but he was good.

'He loved hobnobbing with the great and the famous and in those encounters he could be a very good listener. What important people said really made an impression on him and he tended to believe the last thing any important person said to him. He was very status conscious and aware of who mattered in the world. And, when people were important, he doted on them. When they were on the way down he was happy to give them a good kicking.

'Because he was very intelligent he realised when the wind had changed or he had gone too far. He often bullied women and people who had less power or status than he had. A lot of people were shredded by him. The women who ran his office, he bullied them brutally. Not physically, not sexually, not harassment – just horrible bullying. Reducing them to tears.

'In a meeting, he used to look around and pick on somebody and go for them – it was often a woman but not always.

But when the #MeToo thing happened we noticed him consciously being more polite to people. He started looking for someone and then realised, "I mustn't do that". He had enough self-awareness to preserve himself, to know when he had gone too far and step back. He could even show some compassion once in a while to prove he was a good boss.'

The managing director was demoted and promoted more than once by his chief. The moves seemed arbitrary and he could make as little sense of the promotions as he could the demotions. Once he was able to accept there was no reason for his chief's decisions, he was able to detach himself and not take matters personally. Rather than seeking approval from his boss, he turned to colleagues for praise and confirmation of his good work. Being able to appreciate his chief's intelligence and expertise also helped him cope.

This CEO was skilful in his narcissism. He had enough self-awareness to see how he was perceived by others, which meant he could curtail his destructive behaviour if it impinged on his image as a great leader. This reputation management is of course significantly different from having an interest in others' well-being – the latter being motivated by concern for others, the former by self-interest.

Although we are quick to identify the dangers of a narcissistic leader, it is equally important to recognise the significant contributions they bring to business. Primarily, they have the capacity to attract and inspire followers. Such leaders are often gifted, creative and experts in their field, such as Steve Jobs. They can see the bigger meaning that others miss and possess the optimism and courage to achieve their vision. Because of their need for admiration and even adulation, they tend to be good performers and orators. Even their lack of empathy has an upside as it leaves them free to take tough but necessary decisions – closing a company, for example, or making staff redundant.

The extreme narcissist's insatiable appetite for control, praise and status explains why they strive for and achieve top positions. But while these traits help them climb the career pole, their over-inflated sense of their abilities eventually impairs their judgement. Over-confidence in their own ideas means they do not heed advice or differing views because they think they are cleverer than everyone else.

Kerry Sulkowicz explains that once such individuals reach the top of an organisation, their narcissism worsens by nature of the bubble they find themselves in. The more powerful they are, the less critical feedback they receive and then they are stuck in a loop of their own thinking.

He says: 'There's a lot of praise at the top. As a CEO you're always getting people telling you how good looking and smart you are. What a good job you did. It reinforces their narcissism. That's the danger – it's the 'emperor's new clothes' phenomenon. They start to believe that the praise they're getting is objective and warranted rather than, "I'm getting all this praise because people are kissing my ass and to create favour with me".'

One of the more debilitating consequences of a narcissist at the top is their unwillingness to share the limelight. This can even lead to envious attacks on underlings because seeing others receiving adulation makes them irate. When a company's performance is based on a 'star' CEO, growth and innovation are restricted because subordinates are inhibited from challenging existing ideas or proposing new ones. The chief's unpredictability and volatility instil such fear that staff lose motivation and energy.

Can such people change? That depends on the severity of their narcissism.

Those whose narcissism is less extreme are better equipped to learn and adapt with the help of a good coach or psychotherapist. While their vision, optimism and ability to inspire are assets for a business, these attributes need to be accompanied by a capacity for self-reflection, a determination to control their selfishness and willingness to seek advice when required. They will also need to discard their division of the world into winners and losers and appreciate that strengths and weaknesses reside in us all. For the malignant narcissist, however, change is nearly impossible.

Narcissism is often thought about as a set of behaviours or a personality type but it can also be understood as a protective response to intolerable feelings or trauma, as Dr Bader describes in the case of Trump. Core feelings of shame often originate in early childhood or even infancy when the young child or baby feels helpless against parental neglect, trauma or abuse. The child comes to believe there is something inherently bad about them. These intolerable feelings are pushed down and hidden under a facade of pseudo confidence. The more severe the abuse or neglect, the stronger the armour and the more rigid the defences. Such individuals will resort to extreme measures to keep their confident state alive and repel painful emotions.

Idealisation and devaluation are the common defences they employ. Their need for admiration to cover their deeper feelings of inadequacy and vulnerability are reinforced by devaluing others. They project their unwanted feelings of failure on to unsuspecting targets and this confirms that the unwanted traits lie outside rather than inside them. Essentially, the way such a person boosts their self-esteem is at the expense of others.

Narcissistic parents frequently raise narcissistic children. Their lack of empathy means they are unable to tune into their child's needs and longings, leaving them in a helpless state. They see their children as extensions of themselves rather than unique individuals with their own minds and personalities. Their offspring are evidence of their greatness – 'I must be amazing to have such a remarkable child.' Some narcissistic parents unconsciously project their own unwanted feelings into their children, causing their child to feel like 'the bad one' and thus freeing themselves of their own vulnerability.

This was the case for Paul, a 44-year-old single man from Cambridge, UK. His narcissism was not pathological, as evidenced by the fact that he recognised he had a problem and was seeking help, but it was still worrying enough to cause potentially serious damage to his career and to others. He came to see me when he was newly promoted to a senior role in an events company and found himself struggling with office relationships. On his initial visit, he told me he was having difficulties giving and receiving feedback and that he was taking things personally and becoming overly defensive and occasionally aggressive. This behaviour had become so serious that it had been addressed in a recent review. He worried that his job was at risk.

In a short time we addressed these work issues, but as is often the case, while uncovering what underpinned his aggressive reactions in the office, we touched on deeper matters. These related to his narcissism. Although he had some insight, most concerning was his lack of judgement. He told me how he enjoyed 'getting high' and partying with people he worked with, but he was reluctant to admit the grave danger he was potentially putting himself in, as well as others, both professionally and personally. And although he acknowledged that his reactions could be irrational, another part of him was convinced by his strong feelings. When colleagues presented him with negative feedback or let him down in any way he experienced it as a personal attack that justified a retaliation, or so he believed.

'I always thought that if you don't feel something deeply perhaps you don't care enough,' he said. 'I thought taking it personally was one of my strengths because it meant that I really cared and was passionate about the job. If I get upset about something, I can counter the upset by grabbing on to more positive feelings. There's a cycle of using the good vibes to outweigh the bad – [although] the effect is sometimes the opposite. You can get over-upset about something and it can wipe away the good vibes.'

He desperately craved praise while also fearing criticism that could be piercingly painful. Much of his behaviour was organised around trying to avoid intolerable feelings while ensuring a continuous flow of positive ones.

'I get off on external validation of me, whether it's being seen as a good leader or someone good at their job – but also someone who is fun and behaves like someone younger than they are,' he explained.

His need to impress extended beyond close colleagues to clients and other professional contacts. He needed people to think of him as a contemporary man – engaging, intelligent and fun to be with. To counteract his fears of being rejected or helpless, he sought others to find him interesting and captivating. His convoluted and layered defensive structure distorted reality to the extent that he was reacting inappropriately. In the haze of drug-fuelled connections, he believed there could be a deep and special connection between himself and another.

He justified his actions by insisting they had potentially positive results. 'If I want people to think highly of me it makes me act in a better way [because I want] to maintain the positive feelings people have about me. Particularly with younger people who are more attuned to the quality in the workplace or don't think highly of old-fashioned, slightly misogynistic men.'

He gave an example of a woman he recruited who asked for less money than a male colleague earned in the same position.

'It was tempting to say we'll pay you what you're asking. And I remember saying no, we must offer her the higher amount even though she didn't ask for it because I didn't want to be one of those employers that paid women less than what they were worth. I wanted to tell acquaintances that I had helped to bring about more equality. It was driven by wanting to be seen to be doing the right thing, even more so than actually doing the right thing, if I'm honest. It's partially a narcissistic tendency because a pure altruist would want to have done the right thing regardless of whether anyone else knew.

'I didn't tell her because I'm self-aware enough not to come across as narcissistic by saying how wonderful I am. Sharing it could have backfired. A lot of what drives my thinking is having people see me as a modern male who is not susceptible to sexism and racism, and therefore doing everything to keep that perception more than the reality. That's an example of the power of wanting to create a positive impression of myself so I can take the praise honestly.'

While he wanted to be thought of as an outstanding moral person in the workplace, Paul also wanted to be seen as someone who is up for a good time. Both fed his insatiable need for praise and for people to be interested in him, whether genuine or not.

There was also a manic quality to his behaviour, which is typical of narcissistic personalities. The positive experiences feel enticing, exciting and even risky and these feelings can lift one's mood and keep depressed feelings at bay. Paul's was an internal battle between controlling his selfishness and his need to be admired.

'Can you recall a time you made a bad judgement call because you were seeking someone's admiration?' I asked him.

'Yes,' he responded. 'You can end up getting stoned with someone you shouldn't because you want to keep that vibe going. Or, you strike up an inappropriate friendship where you end up sharing more about your personal life than is professional.

I pressed him further: 'Are you always trying to impress people?'

'That's part of it. Consciously it's about finding people with similar interests. Late-night drinking, partying ... you share stories ... you have that connection. Stuff that's just not work-appropriate.'

Narcissism becomes self-defeating when the person becomes so caught up in creating a marvellous image that they don't see how others see them. The danger was that Paul could become so convinced of his interpretation of events that he believed he could get inside the mind of others and see himself as they viewed him. But his version was more likely to be a projection of his own thoughts and be incorrect – whether assuming people were out to offend him or misreading connections with people as being closer than they were. Both can lead to damaging outcomes.

Both his parents were extreme narcissists who lacked the emotional intelligence to temper their selfishness or recognise the damage they were inflicting on their son. Although he was angry with them for their selfish behaviour, he could not deny the similarities he shared with them.

'Part of me inherited their self-centredness. That's not me being self-deprecating, that's me wrestling with my narcissism. I'm aware enough to know my narcissistic tendencies need tempering.'

He admitted his parents could not see him for who he was and this explains why he craved to be noticed and understood.

'I'm always checking – am I trying to be seen for who I am in a way that my family never did? It was always superficial with them. Providing the basic fundamental necessities of life: clothes, food on the table, are you going to school?, are you alive? Yeah, great, tick the box, good – move on. Not "How are you?" and really mean it and try to understand what's going on beneath the surface. Therefore I do seek deeper connections anywhere I can find them.'

Paul's narcissism resulted from his parents failing to show a genuine interest in him, which left him feeling rejected and shamed. When he experienced criticism or what he perceived as attacks in the workplace, it would ignite those repressed feelings. But there was more. Paul's father had an unpredictable and uncontrollable temper, to which his son fell victim. Much of Paul's behaviour at work was an attempt to control outcomes in order to prevent the kind of rages he experienced as a child. Ensuring people were impressed with him, that they liked him, mitigated the probability he would be attacked.

Over the time we worked together, he showed tremendous courage in examining what lay behind his narcissism. His insight and honesty, but also fears that his poor judgement could damage his career, all contributed to his development. Here he reflects on the changes he has made.

'In the workplace, I have been able to remove the tendency to take things so personally. I have been able to overcome that micromanagement tendency and not be overly annoyed about things not going to plan. I understand that sometimes I was playing out anger which was displaced anger at my parents. The seeking for connections where there might be an ember of connection and then try to push that further – that's still very obvious and it does mean that I sometimes create a friendship with somebody I need to keep a distance from.'

So how should we deal with narcissists who share our workplace? Your first move is to try to identify the type of narcissist you are dealing with.

- Do they appear to have any self-awareness?
- Are they interested in other people other than for their own gain?
- Can they control their emotions?
- Are they willing to listen to alternative views?
- Can they hear critical feedback?

If your answers are an affirmative 'yes,' then you may well be dealing with a productive narcissist and you should feel free to promote ideas and challenge existing ones.

Remember that we all rely on praise and positive regard from others to boost our self-esteem. It is only human to be upset when criticised or when our failures are exposed. Your narcissist is not a monster but likely someone who is more sensitive and emotionally damaged by early trauma. Recognising that behind their confident and charismatic facade lies a bruised and frightened person will help you find some compassion.

One American woman I spoke to empathises with her chief's inexhaustible need for admiration. While he appears to have it all – intelligence, good looks, business success and an enviable lifestyle with residences in Los Angeles, New York and the south of France – she recognises an emptiness in him.

Regarding his narcissism, she says: 'It's as if you have a car with a hole in the tank and you need to fill it all the time because you're losing fuel through the hole. Instead of going to the gas station from time to time, you're having to go on a regular basis. To refuel this need, you need more praise and you need to fuel it indefinitely.'

If your responses to the questions I posed above are a resounding 'no,' however, then you are dealing with an extreme narcissist. In this case, you will need to refer to my 'do's and don'ts' below. As you will see, unfortunately this means putting aside your rational mind and sense of fairness. How you should respond will feel counterintuitive to your better instincts and judgements. You may protest that such advice is unfair; you may believe that a bully needs to be confronted and punished. But think about not what is just and right but rather what will work in your interest. An extreme narcissist is unlikely to change or respond to reasonable requests, so if you must deal with them then it is up to you to adapt. Equally, many of your communication skills will be of little use. And a sycophantic approach will not get you far either – narcissists are often intelligent and if they see you are being disingenuous it can make matters worse. Your aim should be to get the most out of their strengths while preventing unnecessary damage to your self-esteem and professional reputation.

If you find your self-worth has been crushed, you've lost all confidence and/or you find yourself behaving out of character, however, you should consider talking to someone you trust or seeking professional advice to examine if the narcissist has ignited old wounds in you. Alternatively, you may have unconsciously accepted their negative projections and believe you are a loser. Finding someone who can interrupt the self-destructive monologue circulating in your mind can help you see the culprit is not you.

However, do not tolerate abusive behaviour or bullying. If you find the situation intolerable, for the sake of your mental health and well-being, find another job.

Here are my tips for dealing with an extreme narcissist.

**Do not:**

- Ignore them. They are likely to be offended and retaliate.
- Confront them. It could make them paranoid and vindictive.
- Explain yourself. It is likely to receive a condescending response.
- Expect acknowledgement or thanks, nor empathy or interest in you.
- Take criticism from them personally.
- Give in to your instincts to retaliate.
- Express criticism or blame that might injure their self-esteem. When they feel threatened they will attack back.
- Try to explain your point of view. They are unlikely to see it unless it is a version that is to their advantage.

**Do:**

- Be prepared that they will take the credit for your achievements, so keep your expectations low. Realise it is all about their success, not yours.
- Save your energy in trying to get your agenda across. Find out theirs and do your best to go along with it.
- Take advantage of their strengths, appreciate that they can be brilliant and inspiring.
- Begin challenging conversations and critical feedback with praise.
- Keep a record of conversations and events to protect yourself. A narcissist is likely to blame you if things go wrong.
- Look to friends, family and colleagues to boost your self-esteem.
- Show how your ideas suit their purpose.
- Ignore unreasonable requests. In their mania they often deliver a welter of orders that are unachievable.

11

# The upside of the downside – when our neurotic traits come to our rescue

'Only stupid people are happy, because if you can read a newspaper, what is there to be happy about?'

*Alice Shragai*

Alice was my mother. Neither a psychoanalyst nor philosopher, but a proud Jew with more life experience than all psychoanalysts combined, or so I thought when I was young. Her desire was to run the world but she had to live with the disappointment that not many people were hearing her message. 'Why doesn't anyone listen to me?' was her refrain, baffled as to why her global solutions were never taken seriously.

Although she did her best with what fate had dealt her, her life was not a good one. She had little to be happy about yet never became depressed. Which brings me to another of her sayings: 'All the world is on Prozac except me. Don't you think if anyone deserves to go on Prozac, it should be me?' I couldn't argue.

In early 1944, when Alice was just 20, her family were rounded up by Nazi troops together with all other Jews in the city of Kosice, which is now in Slovakia, and deported to Auschwitz. When they stepped off the cattle trains that had carried them for days without food or water, her parents were immediately sent to the right, to the gas chambers, and she to the left. She then spent the remainder of the war as a half-starved slave labourer. After liberation in 1945, she returned home where her hopes of finding someone in her family alive were quickly dashed.

In the ensuing decades, in her mind at least, she never quite left the camps. She was always scared. Whenever my sister and I went to school and my father to work, she found herself back at the dreaded separation point where she last saw her parents. Her intense anger if I was ever late arriving home frightened me. I did not realise it at the time, but it was not me she saw, rather the faces of those she had lost. She talked little of her experiences but what she did say haunted me.

'Everyone who came home from the camps seemed to have someone – a sister, an aunt, a distant cousin even, but I had no one.' While saying this she would raise a clenched fist to an imagined God, as if to say: 'How could you allow this to happen – even if I don't believe in you, I'm furious with you!' Hearing this repeatedly left me with an underlying sadness and deep distrust of humanity.

As a child, I spent hours trying to imagine the scene. How did she travel to Kosice after liberation? When she arrived, where did she sleep? Who gave her clothes, a roof, a bed, something to eat? All these questions swamped my imagination because she said very little. Here is one clue she left me: 'When I arrived in Kosice I passed a tennis court, and a gentile girl shouted at me, "What are you doing here, I thought they killed all of you?" That was my welcome home.'

She seemed always to be agitated. Every time I reprimanded

her for driving me crazy with her irrational rages, her response was the same:

'Don't blame me, blame Hitler.'

Again, I could not argue. I never succeeded in getting my point across because she was undoubtedly the victim, which in turn left me the guilty party. What right had I to inflict further harm on her? I kept silent.

During my early teens, I discovered I could ease her anxieties with gentle understanding. Her anguish far exceeded my needs and so I put them aside to care for her. So began my rehabilitation efforts. This consisted of reintroducing her to what she loved as a child. First, I took her to public gardens to remind her that nature not only housed death camps but could also be a place that soothed. Next, we talked, endlessly. About books, about politics – the Vietnam war, the Watergate trials, but mostly Israel. While she admitted to being 'a communist at heart,' she often voted Republican, insisting this was best for Israel. She was truly a one-off.

I reintroduced her to the theatre and we watched countless comedy shows on television. She even laughed at *Hogan's Heroes* – a sitcom about a POW camp in Nazi Germany. I finally had a functioning mother. Yes, she was damaged, but she also had acute intelligence, profound humanity and a sharp sense of humour. Helping her in this way not only made her less anxious, it also lessened my guilt for any upset I caused.

For as children tend to do, I had quietly absorbed her traumas until they became my own. I became determined to understand how the Holocaust happened while the world watched. When I reached the age she was when deported to

Auschwitz, I began to have strange experiences. I suffered overwhelming grief – inexplicable, because I knew none of the relatives who had died – and an intense hunger and obsession with food that eventually developed into an eating disorder. Not only did I feel the grief she could not face, at less than 90 pounds I looked like a camp inmate myself. When my mind became overwhelmed with images of the Holocaust, my body absorbed what was left. The depression my mother believed she had bypassed was now mine. Perhaps I was the one more equipped to face what had happened because I wasn't the one 'over there.'

Not only did I have her traumas to deal with but I also had my own. Her damage was such that she could not nurture and care for the two daughters she had after liberation. I too suffered some of the highly anxious and chaotic parenting that I have described in this book.

Just as I began to regain my equilibrium, my parents divorced and our family life unravelled. To escape everything, I took another leaf out of my family's book and fled. In the mid-1980s, I went to Europe on a long cycling trip, from which I never returned except for brief visits. Yet alongside the traumas, I had also inherited my parents' strength of survival. I spent all my early adult years running, reinventing and distancing myself from a history that was rich but painful. My parents' history had become my history and it was from this that I fled in order to find a life that was mine.

My years as her 'rehabilitation therapist' not only helped me survive a traumatised mother, they also steered my professional course for years to come. She was the first damaged soul

I helped but by no means would she be the last. Healing broken lives became as natural as breathing.

So the truth is, the trials and tribulations of my childhood ironically gave me an ultimately successful and satisfying career – first as an occupational therapist and hospital programme director, then as an Alexander Technique teacher and psychotherapist and finally as an executive coach. And I am far from alone in benefitting from such an irony. In previous chapters, I have explained and illustrated how early traumas and family dysfunction can impinge on and even severely damage our working lives. Yet there can be a positive side to all this madness and sadness – in many cases, the coping mechanisms we employed to deal with them can prepare us for particular vocations and even help us excel in our careers.

Children can be remarkably creative in finding ways to adapt to a dysfunctional family. The need to imagine one's parents as wonderful, or more caring than they actually are, is powerful. The mind creates psychological defences and behavioural strategies to ensure these beliefs become embedded into a reality of sorts and eventually these coping mechanisms become part of the person's character. Or, as in my case, they find ways to control an otherwise chaotic household. I trod carefully to ease my mother's anxieties and make her less volatile and I successfully took these coping mechanisms into my professional life – albeit with consequences, which I will return to later.

For those who suffered early neglect or abuse, fleeting feelings of being loved or protected in childhood can prove a constant reminder of what is possible. Consequently, the need to draw emotional nourishment from work can be strong, albeit unconscious. Whatever tactics succeeded in gaining the minimum of attention and security amid a tumultuous family life are then employed at work to solve both practical as well as emotional problems. Yet the praise, validation or financial reward for a job well done, no matter how well deserved, never seems to fully satisfy that primal desire.

For many, the tactics learnt in childhood translate into effective skills and behaviour because the motivation to succeed stems directly from early needs for love and security. Such individuals may aspire consciously to succeed, but unconsciously to gain the emotional sustenance they lacked early in life. This combination can produce staggering results, as the examples below suggest.

Richard is an open, polite and warm man in his late thirties. Over the course of our sessions, he described to me how his extreme pleasing behaviour as a child helped him capture the attention of a detached mother, who had little tolerance for his normal childhood moods and bad behaviour. The heightened ability he developed to scrutinise her wishes in order to secure her affection later translated into a facility in reading others and navigating office politics. Anticipating what was needed and getting things done as a child meant that he avoided being excluded from the family fold, and these skills and conduct, when used unconsciously in a professional context, proved extremely successful. His motivation at work went beyond financial incentives and career progression, encompassing a relentless desire for acceptance and security.

He explained to me the theme that ran from boyhood to

manhood: 'When I was very young, I remember doing things to please my mother – cleaning the skirting boards, cooking, getting myself dressed, things that were not what you would expect behaviourally from a kid at that age. That need to please and to create a context where I could get validation from her as manifestation that she loved me is something I now recognise as having had a very positive impact on my career. In situations where there was a need to accommodate difficult office dynamics, I found I was very adept at responding well in order to get things done.'

The response he received from clients and colleagues was always along the lines of: 'We really enjoyed working with you'; 'You have a distinct ability to read a room, manage people's expectations and get a job done'; 'You're always pleasant to work with.'

He became highly adept at second-guessing the emotional responses of others to avoid the rejection he had experienced from his mother.

'Perversely, in a corporate context, that is valued because it's construed as emotional intelligence,' he added.

Another man, Nick, related to me how as a boy he had retreated into his vivid imagination to escape his childhood on a grim London council estate. His parents divorced when he was young, leaving him to look after a clinically depressed mother. His upbringing was understandably gloomy. To escape from this reality, he created a fantasy world of excitement and optimism, even speaking with an American accent to appear more glamorous, such was his need to distance himself from a dispiriting family life. From an early age, he imagined surrounding himself with celebrities – and in so doing, planted the seed for his future career in the entertainment management and marketing industry.

His desire to bolt from the tedium of his youth combined with his fierce ambition led him to establish his own business in this field. As he put it: 'I was fleeing from normality, the everydayness of things. That's why I've never taken a job and always done my own thing.'

His childhood dreamworld had forged an expansive, visionary and creative mind that propelled the success of his company, and his powerful determination enabled him to take necessary risks to develop it. He was not only seeking financial success but also to further banish his childhood misery. Indeed, risk-taking had always felt a necessary part of his escape – it was his anti-depressant.

'When one takes business risks it's easy to post-rationalise and say, "I evaluated all pros and cons,"' he explained. 'More often than not, it comes from the gut – it's part of my DNA to almost want to take risks. The whole purpose of the business we started was to drive the entertainment marketing industry and radically try to change it.'

Reinventing and distancing oneself from a grievous past can be a positive response when it encourages such an optimistic and inventive trajectory. It does not dismiss your past but adds to it in a way that is both rich and uniquely yours. The stories we tell ourselves largely inform not only how we perceive ourselves but also what we believe to be possible. As with Nick, we have the potential to write our own narrative and this can enhance our professional lives. We cannot have a successful future unless we can imagine it.

For many, the motivation to succeed coupled with an underlying incentive to recreate one's life story is a powerful combination. The drive to ensure one is not forgotten or to feel secure is as strong, if not more so, than desire for financial or professional achievement. The following case illustrates how far a longing to flee and the ability to reinvent oneself can take you.

Keith was in his early thirties and had been working for a public relations company for three years when he asked to see me. He was prompted to do so after reading an article of mine in the *Financial Times* about confusing professional relationships with intimacy. An articulate and attractive man, he was well dressed and exuded charm. We soon clicked. I was struck particularly by how effortlessly he put me at ease, when usually it is the coach or therapist who should perform that role. Our ensuing conversations would shed light on this initial encounter.

'What was it about the article that struck a chord with you?' I asked.

He quickly let his guard down to divulge his worry. The company he had been working for had recently taken a turn for the worse. He knew he had to leave but was extremely anxious about his boss's reaction. Although they had a close working relationship, Keith worried that his boss would be furious and hit the roof when he heard the news.

Their relationship had begun a few years previously when they met at another company. Keith had impressed him with his intellect and business savvy, so when his boss left the company he took Keith with him. Through their collective endeavour in forming the new company Keith won him over entirely and his chief soon became extremely dependent upon him. Keith soon discovered how to 'work' him and convince him to do things his way.

He explained: 'On the rational side, you couldn't convince him unless you had a watertight case. On the emotional side, I was very tuned into his moods and concerns and matched my approach based on that. You had to pick your timing and make sure he was in the right mood. At times he could be rude, shouting at me in front of peers. He'd ask me to get him a latte even though I was doing all the work and he was not doing anything. That said, I was treated better than everyone else. He listened to me, I was involved in all the decisions, I got whatever I wanted. I was his favourite.'

When it came to the crunch point, Keith was enormously relieved that he was able to convince his boss to make him redundant. 'I led him to that conclusion very slowly. It became his idea and his decision, and therefore he had the control and my exit was fine.'

Keith's ability to read people and situations was the driving force behind his professional success. 'I've always been able to get a sense of people relatively quickly. You can tell if they're interested or not by the way they look. You can tell who doesn't like who. If someone is insecure, what might you do to make them feel good? Or, if someone wants to feel in control or the most important person in the room, I'd be very aware of that. I can have a sense that he wants to be the one in charge – or she doesn't feel like anyone ever listens to her.'

He explained that he tended to have a detached reaction to

people, in which he asked himself: 'What are their needs and I'll adapt to that.'

'They tend to do what you want them to do if you're able to work out what their emotional needs are. By and large, I work them for my advantage. It's just more practical. I tend to be more successful with more senior people than peers.'

'Can you say more about how you learnt this?' I asked.

'I guess because I was bullied a lot at school, so I think I had to learn how to avoid arousing anger in people. There were times I didn't have a lot of friends, so I was careful not to say the wrong thing in case I had this disproportionate reaction where no one would speak to me. I found myself in situations in my childhood and teenage years where I had to manage the moods of other people because if I got something wrong or upset them, I would get beaten up. So I had to be very attuned to people's temperaments – what they said, what they didn't say. I veered toward the catastrophic possibility; what would happen if they were in a bad mood.'

And he added: 'In business you can do quite well by never fucking up. You don't necessarily need to go in with guns blazing, you just have to avoid a catastrophe – especially in corporate life.'

I was curious as to why he was more successful with people senior to him than his peers. I wondered if unconsciously it was his father's attention he hoped to capture.

'I imagine the first person who had power over you was your father,' I suggested.

'Yes, I guess that would have been the original one. He could lose his temper at any point. Because I couldn't predict his temper, I was very vigilant.'

'Could you say more about your father? How did you feel about him?'

Keith explained that he came from a working-class family in Liverpool where money was usually tight.

'[My father] wanted to be a good dad but unfortunately his temper got the better of him. He lost it on too many occasions and that damaged our relationship. There were times I did try to do things with him but he didn't want to do that much. He worked long hours in a factory and was often exhausted. He found having four children stressful. We were often broke and he found having money problems very stressful. And, I think he didn't have a good upbringing himself and didn't have a template of how to be a dad.'

'Are you trying to capture your boss's attention the way you tried to gain your father's?' I asked

'Yeah. I think at some time I must have got praise for having done well at school so then I tried to do well as a way of getting praise. But later on, that backfired because I think they didn't want me to shine too brightly because my siblings might feel bad, so that didn't work.'

He eventually succeeded by creating a life far removed from the distress he experienced in his youth, as he explained.

'I didn't fit in at all. I was an academic kid, very effeminate and sensitive and I was in a very rough state school in a bad part of Liverpool. I was desperately unhappy. I didn't want to be anything like the people I grew up with, I didn't want to be anything like my dad. The only way I could see of getting out of it was university. All my drive was with the intention of getting out of there.

'Then I went about changing myself. I changed my accent, I changed the way I looked, then I moved to London and I learnt very quickly that you can't really be working-class and have a good career, so I learnt to affect middle-class ways and learnt how to deal with middle-class people.

'I remember learning quickly that people like similar people, and if you're not similar they don't like you. So, I learnt ways – such as lying – of fitting in. I never talked about my school and people just projected their assumptions on to me. Everyone assumed I went to private schools and I never corrected them. I thought, "I'll just fit in to whatever you think I should be." If they thought I was boring and stable, I was quite happy with that because I think those were their values. They're like horses, they get scared quite easily. So I try to keep in line with what they want to hear.'

While his early coping strategies helped him escape a miserable childhood and later gain financial success, I asked him if there was a price to pay, either professionally or personally. He admitted that because he treated work relationships as more transactional, he had not formed friendships at work and at times felt lonely. But the real cost, he said, was personal rather than professional. He has worked so hard to hone an image that he now found it difficult to know who his authentic self was. It had also become harder for him to relate to and empathise with people. While this suits business relationships, it can of course hinder personal ones.

'That's the drawback. I've become very functional rather than just a person. If someone else can tell me how to have a better quality of life not coming from a privileged background,

I'm open to it. But I don't see – unless you are a footballer – how you do it.'

He had been very successful at crafting an identity that he believed his colleagues, clients and superiors would feel most comfortable with, but at the expense of his sense of self. Treating work relationships as transactional protected him – how could anyone hurt him if they never knew who he was?

Keith was able to sustain a strong armour until his boss triggered his deeper longings and fears. The attention he missed from his father he now wished from his boss. While he worked enormously hard to win his boss's admiration, it was contingent on certain behaviour. Once he retreated, in this case for another job, he feared the admiration, or love as he perceived it, would be withdrawn.

In truth, he had not distanced himself from his past as much as he believed. His boss, like his father, was a bully. Remember that our determination to return to the familiar can overtake our conscious wishes. It would be reasonable to hypothesise that his unconscious had played a part in recreating similar humiliating experiences at work as in his childhood. We concluded that while he had travelled a long way in some respects, in others he had not gone far. Those situations that we flee from are often the ones that we unconsciously recreate.

It is a popular notion to link early traumatic experiences to people's success. The loss of a parent in early life, Malcolm Gladwell claims in his 2008 book, *The Outliers: The Story of Success,* can propel people to chart their own ambitious way – a category Gladwell calls 'eminent orphans.' The fact that 12 American presidents lost their fathers while they were young is often cited, too. And historian Lucille Iremonger recorded as far back as 1970 in her book *Fiery Chariot: A Study of British Prime Ministers and the Search for Love* that 67 per cent of British prime ministers from the beginning of the nineteenth century to the Second World War lost a parent before the age of 16.

The term 'post-traumatic growth' refers to the positive life changes that can occur when overcoming adversity. There is no doubt that confronting catastrophe can make us stronger and more resilient. Yet while it might be comforting to hear such 'success' stories, they often fail to reveal the contrasting side. That is, what has helped these individuals survive may also have impinged on their lives. This does not diminish the fact that some people have an extraordinary ability to flourish after traumatic experiences. The experience, however, is more complex than at face value.

As we have seen in many of the case studies in this book, early coping mechanisms are not only attempts at gaining much needed security but also ways to control events in our immediate environment. Pleasing a parent or learning to be agreeable can keep the emotional temperature at home at a manageable level. In the workplace, the same strategies can be used to control outcomes. Extreme and compulsive work behaviour, for example, can also be understood in this way. 'If I work hard enough or avoid any mistakes, I will be successful and therefore avoid negative consequences.'

For many, however, the compulsion to work hard is so extreme as to result in workaholism, obsessive-compulsive behaviour or burnout. While professional results might be positive, the price is often damage to personal relationships. Focusing entirely on work or achievement can be a defence, for example, against the strong feelings that are aroused in close relationships. For some it is far easier to control work outcomes than the emotional turmoil of intimacy.

Undoubtedly my early experiences strengthened me. The downside was that the only way I allowed myself to be close to people was by making myself useful to them, as I had with my mother. Intimacy scared me – I had to learn how to have a real relationship. And determined to be self-sufficient, I found it difficult to accept help when I was the one in serious need.

Finding oneself in such a quandary need not compromise one's career – on the contrary, it can also be a creative and revitalising space. It allows one to pause, reflect and consider other possibilities. Such dilemmas can create conflicts and paralyse people but can also be transformative if one is willing to face the past and examine options for the future.

As regards people whose traits have brought them success but then become obstacles to further career progression, I encourage them to face the consequences of continuing these characteristics. Where people-pleasing helps create allies and avoid conflicts, for example, the wish to be liked can interfere with making tough, sometimes unpopular decisions. Controlling behaviour that at a lower level gets things done, at more senior strata it can stifle risk-taking and innovative thinking. Perfectionism that protected you against severe scoldings in childhood as well as criticism in the workplace eventually cannot be sustained because of the sheer energy required. Going with the flow might have been useful to step around a domineering parent and be a good team member but being creative and standing out requires not holding back for fear of being judged.

Precisely because these traits are inextricably bound with early coping mechanisms makes it difficult to change. And even when these strategies no longer work, people return to them with yet more vigour. But problems arise when your coping mechanisms have become your sole solution to solving every work problem. Often something happens. Perhaps one suffers burnout or a work assessment is devastating in its criticism. Perhaps you are identified as someone with poor interpersonal skills or are assailed by underlings for having unrealistic expectations of them. Maybe the turning point begins at home. Your spouse complains that you are irritable and distant or you recognise that your children are growing quickly and you are missing their best years. Perhaps your health is deteriorating, your blood pressure is too high and stress-related ailments too frequent.

You see the risks and dangers of continuing but are compelled to push on. If you have always relied on a particular strategy – whether it is people-pleasing, obsessive behaviour, perfectionism or, in my case, rescuing – it will obviously be difficult to change. Shedding these strategies may give rise to repressed feelings from childhood. You might have to face who your parents actually were as opposed to who you imagined them to be. There may be some grief and sadness as a result. Other emotions might arise, perhaps the guilt or rage you repressed and disguised behind your pleasing behaviour. When I stopped caring for my mother, for example, I felt the years of anger that I never expressed for fear of hurting her.

Then there is the nagging fear: 'If I let go of my habitual

behaviour will I fail? Will everything I achieved so far be lost?' If you believe your success has resulted from the strength of your survival strategies alone, your mind might take you on a spiralling, catastrophic thought train until you imagine yourself homeless and destitute.

I often reassure people that it is unnecessary to give up these tactics entirely – nor is it realistic to believe you can. It is far more comforting to know that you can always rely on them if need be. I suggest you learn to manage them skilfully while developing other ways of responding. That is, there will be occasions where perfectionism, obsessiveness, people-pleasing or even rescuing will be useful. The trick is to know when it is helpful as opposed to harmful and develop ways of consciously managing these traits.

I would not want to give up being compassionate and empathic, I like helping people. These are positive qualities and only become harmful when I ignore my own needs. To grow personally and professionally, however, I had to examine my early life. It was far easier to allow others to depend on me because it ensured I was never the vulnerable one. But I also had to learn to rely on others – and that felt much riskier.

For many, the consequences of persisting with historic coping strategies are felt more in personal than professional relationships. Compulsive work habits take away one's attention from family and intimate relationships. The cost to one's career advancement, however, is normally experienced at times of promotion or transition, when the traits one has relied on no longer work, or even make things worse.

Richard, the man who worked excessively hard to capture

his mother's attention, described how the same unbridled habits eventually led to more problems, rather than resolutions, in the workplace. The more hypersensitive he was to others, the less emotional bandwidth he had for himself. With his antenna directed more outward than inward, he became detached from his needs and feelings, relying ever more on others to reassure him. His natural inclination was to work harder to rectify any problematic situation, even when these attempts were not working, not realising that the problem might lie with the organisation rather than him. The price he paid was losing an ability to think imaginatively and creatively, to be brave and do things differently.

'If someone says you've done a good job, that's qualitatively different than being told that you're loved,' he explained. 'For many years, I didn't have the psychological understanding of that distinction. It's not the responsibility of the people you work with to give you that [love]. The response that's needed in a corporate context is one of cool objectivity and the need to stand back and give a dispassionate view. If your judgement is clouded by an unconscious need to be validated, that can detract from your ability to exercise good strategic and professional judgement.'

Our most challenging moments at work often remind us of what remains unresolved from our past. It is a nudge to pause and reflect. This process is not a quick fix by any means – it takes time. There is no obvious end or clear markers along the way. People who have come to me are often impatient. I am reminded of another of my mother's sayings: 'If you live long enough, everything comes to you.'

# 12

# Will work ever love me back?

'I never understood why happy people bother getting out of bed.'

This was a line in my comedy stand-up set. At the time, I truly could not fathom what motivated happy people. While I wished to improve my performance, be successful and make people laugh, my deeper motivation was to rid myself of unhappiness. I was fleeing loneliness, looking for a place to be seen and belong and trying to fill my life with distractions so as not to face what I believed was my unlovability. When an audience responds to your performance with roars of laughter, it is not difficult to construe that you are lovable. This was powerful enough to make me return to the comedy circuit again and again, even after the odd devastating performance.

Although stand-up comedy offers an extreme example of seeking love from work, the desire is ubiquitous. Work confronts us with our deepest longings and fears. Will I be accepted and appreciated? Will I be understood? We all crave to be heard, to belong and, ultimately, to be loved. But is the answer to the question, 'Will work ever love me back', really 'Yes'? The answer, I believe, is neither a resounding yes or no but rather lies in the grey area in between.

Some fortunate people when asked this question will

positively raise their hands in an affirmative 'Yes!' because they find their occupation endlessly gratifying and rewarding, beyond merely developing professionally and gaining financial security. Work can offer meaning, a sense of being part of something bigger than ourselves, as well as a place to explore our talents and interests. For others who struggle with underlying feelings of inadequacy or lack belief in their lovability, work can acquire a yet more profound meaning. It can become a place to prove your past wrong, to acquire the much desired praise that had previously been lacking or to seek the safety, security and love that was absent or only fleeting in childhood. And for those who struggle with intimacy, or find themselves without a partner or family, it offers a substitute – a kind of pseudo intimacy in place of the real thing.

These benefits are not to be dismissed – for many they can spell the difference between acute loneliness and a work life rich in meaning and companionship. Work can also provide a safety net for those who are extremely fearful or insecure. The structure can provide grounding in contrast to the internal chaos they experience. The success of and praise from a job well done, a deserved promotion or just the sheer pleasure of finding satisfaction in a career all boost one's self-worth and can even rewrite a narrative distinct from what has gone before.

But a warning for people who rely on their occupation entirely for their emotional nourishment. What happens come retirement, or if the job ends abruptly when the company either collapses or makes them redundant? Suddenly the great bulwark of their life is swept away and they are left alone and bereft.

The same applies to those obsessed solely with garnering the financial rewards of work to gain concrete evidence of their worth. Accumulating wealth proves only that one can succeed in becoming rich; it does little to confirm one's lovability. If a certain level of wealth could make you feel accepted and successful, all well and good. But with money, the bar is usually forever being raised. It is precisely being caught in a cycle of 'never enough' that signals the disappointing truth that the craving to be admired, to be loved or repair historic hurts cannot be attained through financial success. Added to this can be overachievement, perfectionism, workaholism and other psychological traits examined in this book. When one is forever craving more, when the project is never 'good enough', achievements are quickly forgotten and praise never penetrates enough to alter one's feelings of self-worth then it must be said, 'work will not love you back'.

This is not to suggest that work cannot correct historic harms and hurts. Appreciate your accomplishments, accept praise without dismissing it and acknowledge that the odd setback does not wipe out all previous successes. Let work boost your self-worth and belief, and then yes, it can love you back. This requires shifting one's mindset – by no means a simple task. It requires the kind of self-examination I have explained to identify the source of one's wrong thinking.

To change we need to be grounded in reality and inhibit the tendency to allow our past to colour our reading of current events. To navigate through the psychological thicket that work can present us with, it is essential to regard it as a relationship that has limits, is finite and can, like any human relationship, disappoint and frustrate. While it provides opportunities to meet our emotional needs, perspective is vital. Let me stress that work and personal relationships are significantly different. While those at work are predominantly transactional, intimate ones are much deeper and provide more tolerance for our vulnerabilities. Both, however, contain risk – innovation risks failure, closeness risks being hurt and rejection is always a possibility.

To protect ourselves in the workplace, we talk about 'colleagues,' 'bosses' and 'direct reports' as if they were not real relationships. While this helps to secure boundaries between people, it implies that we should not be needy of them or feel strongly one way or the other about them – but of course we generally do. Yet while work provokes strong feelings, there is little tolerance in the workplace for their existence. Expression of emotion is allowed only within limits. This is understandable and reasonable in terms of efficiency and regulation of behaviour but it leaves many individuals confused and overwhelmed by emotions that cannot be expressed, addressed and therefore understood. And paradoxically, aspects of our performance rely on them. Being passionate, imaginative, relating and empathising with others, all require tuning into our emotions. Yet simultaneously, there is this intolerance for feelings, a belief we should keep them to ourselves and be 'professional.' It seems work wants our 'good' feelings but doesn't allow for our 'bad' ones. It is our responsibility to bridge this gap and take the time to develop ways to not only manage but also make sense of our emotional lives.

It is up to us to gain as much control over our unconscious as possible to limit its potential damage in the workplace. If, for example, the illusion sets in that the boss cares more for you than he or she actually does, the obsession to retain that attention can overtake your capacity to think objectively and take sound decisions. We need to be aware of how, unintentionally, we might be creating the very situations we are trying to avoid by misreading matters or applying a historic template to present events.

Bringing our unconscious motivations to conscious awareness is particularly crucial at a time when the fast-changing nature of work demands even more of our psychological strength. The gig economy and rapid technological development result in less security, and remote working during and after the pandemic has altered how we relate to each other. The opportunities for passing moments that offer acknowledgement, reassurance and advice, or random conversations that trigger breakthrough ideas, have been reduced. Individuals will need the emotional maturity to navigate the many insecurities, uncertainties and setbacks that inevitably will arise. Tolerating strong and uncomfortable feelings, having the insight to distinguish past from present and the courage and imagination to adapt your response to new circumstances will leave you better equipped to succeed in your career.

We visit the past not to be attached to it but rather to be free from it. While stressing the need for personal awareness and insight, to have any real worth it must be translated into change and action. Such examination will give us a future that, rather than resembling our past, allows us to create a life that is uniquely ours.

# Acknowledgements

The roots of this book go back some 15 years when my clients and I began examining the unconscious themes behind their business-related problems. Together we discovered how their inner lives informed their working practices, and seeing their professional and personal lives transformed as a result was immensely satisfying. Their intention in contributing to this book has been solely to help others by sharing their stories. I feel very grateful and privileged to have benefited from their honesty and integrity. Without them this book would not have been possible.

Early inspiration from these clients prompted me to approach the *Financial Times.* At that time, the paper had published next to nothing about people's emotional lives, but my first article – about fathers struggling to balance work and home life – struck a chord with Ravi Mattu, editor of the Business Life section, and with readers, too. Ravi then took a risk by inviting a relatively inexperienced writer to contribute regularly. I owe him much thanks, and also to my current editor at the *Financial Times,* Isabel Berwick, for her interest in, and support of my work.

While writing features for the FT I was fortunate to interview many executives, business advisers, academics, psychoanalysts, psychologists and thinkers who have not only enhanced my professional development but also contributed to this book. I am grateful to all of them. In particular, Kerry Sulkowicz immediately impressed me with his experience, intelligence and application of psychoanalysis to business. We clicked instantly and began a successful collaborative working relationship that developed into a warm friendship. Much gratitude also to Manfred Kets de Vries. His many books, wealth of articles and wisdom have been inspirational. Michael Bader has shown me, through his writing, how complex psychodynamic ideas can be made accessible and compelling for readers. He has also been consistently generous in responding to my questions.

I would never have found the time, energy or courage to write this book had I not been approached by my Penguin editor, Drummond Moir. He had an idea for a book – how people's working lives are influenced by their early family experiences – and sought me out on the strength of my FT articles. We quickly found that we were on the same page and so began an illuminating and exhilarating working relationship. His insights and suggestions have improved every chapter, while copy editor Liz Marvin's contributions and suggestions made them an easier and more logical read. Others at Penguin who have contributed to this book are unknown to me, yet deserve my deepest thanks. Added to this list must be my friend and personal reader, Alison Williams, whose meticulous reading of each chapter identified useful corrections. Thank you Ali.

Others contributed by generously taking the time to be interviewed and sharing their knowledge and experience: Margaret Heffernan, David Tuckett, Peter Fonagy, Alexandra

Michel, Laura Empson, Kenneth Eisold, Roshni Raveendhran, Steve Axelrod, Sally-Ann Tschanz, Niels Van Quaquebeke and Greg Hodder. Josh Cohen helped me think through some of the case examples and added to my understanding. Special thanks also to those who contributed anonymously.

I am not the most confident of writers and require encouragement. Fortunately, my husband Charlie was unfailing in this regard. It is no exaggeration to say that not much would happen without his unshakeable support and belief in me. He is a saint.

When writing one's first book, it is useful to have a cheerleader or two. Luckily I had an excessive supply in friends and family members. They are too numerous to mention, but I deeply appreciate their good wishes and interest. Special thanks, however, to my lifelong friend Mark Matousek, who always encouraged me to write.

# Bibliography

Anderson, C., Sharps, D.L., Soto, C.J., and John, O.P. 'People with disagreeable personalities (selfish, combative, and manipulative) do not have an advantage in pursuing power at work.' *PNAS*, (2020), Vol. 117, No. 37, 22780-22786

Axelrod, Steven. *Work and the Evolving Self* (New Jersey, The Analytic Press, 1999)

Bader, Michael. 'Secrets and Lies: Decoding the Dangerous Mind of Donald Trump.' *The Medium*, Feb 29 2020

Chatterjee, A. and Hambrick, D.C. 'Executive Personality, Capability Cues, and Risk Taking: How Narcissistic CEOs React to Their Successes and Stumbles.' *Administrative Science Quarterly*, (2011), Vol. 56, No. 2, 202–237

Duffy M., Scott K., Shaw J., Tepper B., Aquino K. 'A Social Context Model of Envy and Social Undermining.' *Academy of Management Journal* (2012)

Eddy, Bill and DiStefano, L.Georgi. *It's All Your Fault at Work: Managing Narcissists and Other High Conflict People* (Unhooked Books, 2015)

Empson, Laura. *Leading Professionals: Power, Politics, and Prima Donnas* (Oxford University Press, 2017)

Garland, Caroline. *Understanding Trauma: A Psychoanalytic Approach* (Karnac, 2002)

Gladwell, Malcolm. *Outliers: The Story of Success* (Penguin Books, 2009)

Goslett, Miles. 'Kid's Company: How the Spectator first blew the whistle,' *The Spectator*, 1 February 2016

Heffernan, M. *Wilful Blindness* (Simon and Schuster, 2019)

Heffernan, M. *Unchartered* (Simon and Schuster, 2020)

Hirschhorn, Larry. *The Workplace Within: Psychodynamics of Organizational Life* (The MIT Press, 1988)

Hopper, Earl. *Trauma and Organizations* (Karnac Books, 2012)

Iremonger, Lucille. *Fiery Chariot: A Study Of British Prime Ministers and the Search for Love* (Martin Secker & Warburg, 1970)

Kahn, Susan. *Death and the City: On Loss, Mourning, and Melancholia at Work* (Karnac Books, 2017)

Kellaway, Kate. 'Patrick Marber: I'll be in therapy for the rest of my life if I can afford it', *Guardian*, March 7 2020

Kets de Vries, Manfred F.R. 'The Dangers of Feeling Like a Fake', *HBR Magazine*, September 2005

Kets de Vries, Manfred F.R. *The Leader on the Couch: A clinical approach to changing people and organisations* (Jossey-Bass, 2012)

Kets de Vries, Manfred F.R. *Down the Rabbit Hole of Leadership: Leadership Pathology in Everyday Life* (France: Palgrave Macmillan, 2019)

Kramer, Roderick, M. 'Paranoid Cognition in Social Systems: Thinking and Acting in the Shadow of Doubt.' *Personality and Social Psychology Review*, (1998), Vol. 2, No. 4, 251-275

Kramer, Roderick M. 'When Paranoia Makes Sense'. *HBR Magazine*, July 2002

McWilliams, Nancy. *Psychoanalytic Diagnosis: Understanding Personality Structure in the Clinical Process* (New York and London: The Guilford Press, 2011)

Maccoby, Michael. 'Narcissistic Leaders: The Incredible Pros, the Inevitable Cons.' *HBR Magazine*, January 2004

Maccoby, Michael. 'Why People Follow the Leader: The Power of Transference.' *HBR Magazine*, September 2004

Menon, T. and Thompson, L. 'Envy at Work', *HBR Magazine*, April 2010

Michel, A. 'Participation and Self-Entrapment: A 12-Year Ethnography of Wall Street Participation Practices' Diffusion and Evolving Consequences.' *The Sociological Quarterly*, (2014), Vol. 55, 514-536

Michel, A. 'Transcending socialization: A nine-year ethnography of the body's role in organizational control and knowledge workers' transformation.' *Administrative Science Quarterly*, (2011), Vol 56, No. 3, 325-368

Milliken, Frances J., Morrison, Elizabeth W., Hewlin, Patricia F. 'An Exploratory Study of Employee Silence: Issues that Employees Don't Communicate Upward and Why.' *Journal of Management Studies*, (2003), Vol. 40, No. 6, 1453-76

Milliken, Frances J. and Morrison, Elizabeth W., 'Organizational Silence: A Barrier to Change and Development in a Pluralistic World', *Academy of Management Review*, (2000), Vol. 25, No. 4

Obholzer, Anton and Roberts, Vega Zagier eds. *The Unconscious at Work: A Tavistock Approach to Making Sense of Organizational Life* (London and New York: Routledge, 2019)

Raveendhran, R. 'Micromanagement: Misunderstood?'. *Businessworld*, January 2019

Reh, S., Tröster, C. and Van Quaquebeke, N. 'Keeping (Future) Rivals Down: Temporal Social Comparison Predicts Coworker Social Undermining via Future Status Threat and Envy.' *Journal of Applied Psychology*, (2018), Vol. 103, No. 4, 399-415

Ruppert, Franz. *Trauma, Bonding and Family Constellations* (UK: Green Balloon Publishing, 2008)

Shragai, Naomi. 'How the children of working parents can thrive.' *Financial Times.* 16 May 2017

Shragai, Naomi. 'How not to worship your boss.' *Financial Times*, 26 July 2016

Shragai, Naomi. 'The fear of being found out.' *Financial Times*, 4 September 2013

Shragai, Naomi. 'Life with a narcissistic manager.' *Financial Times*, 28 October 2013

Shragai, Naomi. 'Paranoia at work is out to get you.' *Financial Times*, 17 July 2014

Shragai, Naomi. 'Surviving the success of others.' *Financial Times*, 16 April 2014

Shragai, Naomi. 'What drives an overachiever at work?'. *Financial Times*, 19 September 2018

Stein, Mark. 'When Does Narcissistic Leadership Become Problematic? Dick Fuld at Lehman Brothers', *Journal of Management Inquiry*, (2013), Vol. 22, No. 3, 282-293

Stein, Mark. 'Envy and Leadership.' *European Journal of Work and Organizational Psychology*, (1997), Vol. 6, No. 4, 453-465

Storr, Farrah. 'Why Imposter Syndrome is Every Woman's Weapon.' *Elle*, 9 June 2019

Tuckett, D. and Taffler, R.J., *Fund Mangement: An Emotional Finance Perspective* (London: The Research Foundation of CFA Institute, 2012)

Tedlow, R.S., 'Leaders in Denial.' *HBR Magazine*, July–August 2008

Van Quaquebeke, Niels. 'Paranoia as an Antecedent and Consequence of Getting Ahead in Organizations: Time-Lagged Effects Between Paranoid Cognitions, Self-Monitoring, and Changes in Span of Control.' *Frontiers in Psychology*, (2016), Vol. 7, 1446

Vaughan Smith, Julia. *Coaching and Trauma: From surviving to thriving* (London: Open University Press, 2019)

Williams, Z. 'Jenny Eclair: "Menopause gave me incandescent rage. It was like a superpower."' *Guardian*, 20 June 2020

Wright, P.M., Cragun, O.R., Nyberg, A.J., Schepker, D.J., Ulrich, M.D. 'CEO Narcissism, CEO Humility and C-Suite Dynamics.' *Center for Executive Succession*, (2016)

# Index

# Index

Stephen Linehan